TITUS ANDRONICUS

WILLIAM SHAKESPEARE

Published by True Sign Publishing House
Address: SY. No. 21/2 & 21/3, Sonnenahalli,
Krishnarajapura, Bengaluru,
Karnataka - 560049 India
E-mail: truesignbooks@gmail.com
Website: www.truesign.in

Titus Andronicus

Author: William Shakespeare

ISBN: 978-93-5462-758-3

First Edition: 2022

Contents

Dramatis Personæ

Saturninus—	son to the late Emperor of Rome, afterwards Emperor.
Bassianus—	brother to Saturninus.
Titus Andronicus—	a noble Roman.
Marcus Andronicus—	Tribune of the People, and brother to Titus.
Lucius, Quintus, Martius, Mutius—	sons to Titus Andronicus.
Young Lucius	a boy, son to Lucius.
Publius	son to Marcus Andronicus.
Sempronius, Caius, Valentine—	kinsmen to Titus.
Aemilius	a noble Roman.
Alarbus, Demetrius, Chiron—	sons to Tamora.
Aaron, a Moor—	beloved by Tamora.
A Captain.	
A Messenger.	
A Clown.	
Tamora—	Queen of the Goths.
Lavinia—	daughter to Titus Andronicus.

A Nurse, and a black Child.

Romans and Goths, Senators, Tribunes, Officers, Soldiers, and Attendants.

Scene: Rome and the neighbourhood.

ACT-1

SCENE-1— Rome. Before the Capitol

The Tomb of the ANDRONICI *appearing; the Tribunes and Senators aloft. Enter, below, from one side,* SATURNINUS *and his Followers; and, from the other side,* BASSIANUS *and his Followers; with drum and colours*

SATURNINUS

Noble patricians, patrons of my right, Defend the justice of my cause with arms,And, countrymen, my loving followers,Plead my successive title with your swords:I am his first-born son, that was the lastThat wore the imperial diadem of Rome;Then let my father's honours live in me,Nor wrong mine age with this indignity.

BASSIANUS

Romans, friends, followers, favorers of my right,
If ever Bassianus, Caesar's son,Were gracious in the eyes of royal Rome,Keep then this passage to the CapitolAnd suffer not dishonour to approachThe imperial seat, to virtue consecrate,To justice, continence and nobility;But let desert in pure election shine,And, Romans, fight for freedom in your choice.

Enter MARCUS ANDRONICUS, *aloft, with the crown*

MARCUS ANDRONICUS

Princes, that strive by factions and by friends
Ambitiously for rule and empery,Know

that the people of Rome, for whom we standA special party, have, by common voice,In election for the Roman empery,Chosen Andronicus, surnamed PiusFor many good and great deserts to Rome:A nobler man, a braver warrior,Lives not this day within the city walls:He by the senate is accit'd homeFrom weary wars against the barbarous Goths;That, with his sons, a terror to our foes,Hath yoked a nation strong, train'd up in arms.Ten years are spent since first he undertookThis cause of Rome and chastised with armsOur enemies' pride: five times he hath return'dBleeding to Rome, bearing his valiant sonsIn coffins from the field;And now at last, laden with horror's spoils,Returns the good Andronicus to Rome,Renowned Titus, flourishing in arms.Let us entreat, by honour of his name,Whom worthily you would have now succeed.And in the Capitol and senate's right,Whom you pretend to honour and adore,That you withdraw you and abate your strength;Dismiss your followers and, as suitors should,Plead your deserts in peace and humbleness.

SATURNINUS

How fair the tribune speaks to calm my thoughts!

BASSIANUS

Marcus Andronicus, so I do ally
In thy uprightness and integrity,And so I love and honour thee and thine,Thy noble brother Titus and his sons,And her to whom my thoughts are humbled all,Gracious Lavinia, Rome's rich ornament,That I will here dismiss my loving friends,And to my fortunes and the people's favorCommit my cause in balance to be weigh'd.

Exeunt the followers of BASSIANUS

SATURNINUS Friends, that have been thus forward in my right,
I thank you all and here dismiss you all,And to the love and favor of my countryCommit myself, my person and the cause.

Exeunt the followers of SATURNINUS

Rome, be as just and gracious unto me
As I am confident and kind to thee.Open the gates, and let me in.

BASSIANUS Tribunes, and me, a poor competitor.

Flourish. SATURNINUS *and* BASSIANUS *go up into the Capitol*

Enter a CAPTAIN

CAPTAIN Romans, make way: the good Andronicus.
Patron of virtue, Rome's best champion,Successful in the battles that he fights,With honour and with fortune is return'dFrom where he circumscribed with his sword,And brought to yoke, the enemies of Rome.

Drums and trumpets sounded. Enter MARTIUS *and* MUTIUS; *After them, two Men bearing a coffin covered with black; then* LUCIUS *and* QUINTUS. *After them,* TITUS ANDRONICUS; *and then* TAMORA, *with* ALARBUS, DEMETRIUS, CHIRON, AARON, *and other Goths, prisoners; Soldiers and people following. The Bearers set down the coffin, and* TITUS *speaks*

TITUS ANDRONICUS Hail, Rome, victorious in thy mourning weeds!
Lo, as the bark, that hath discharged her fraught,Returns with precious jading to the bayFrom whence at first she weigh'd her anchorage,Cometh Andronicus, bound with laurel boughs,To re-salute his country with his tears,Tears of true joy for his return to Rome.Thou great defender of this Capitol,Stand gracious to the rites that we intend!Romans, of five and twenty valiant sons,Half of the number that King

Priam had,Behold the poor remains, alive and dead!These that survive let Rome reward with love;These that I bring unto their latest home,With burial amongst their ancestors:Here Goths have given me leave to sheathe my sword.Titus, unkind and careless of thine own,Why suffer'st thou thy sons, unburied yet,To hover on the dreadful shore of Styx?Make way to lay them by their brethren.

The tomb is opened

There greet in silence, as the dead are wont,
And sleep in peace, slain in your country's wars!O sacred receptacle of my joys,Sweet cell of virtue and nobility,How many sons of mine hast thou in store,That thou wilt never render to me more!

LUCIUS

Give us the proudest prisoner of the Goths,
That we may hew his limbs, and on a pileAd manes fratrum sacrifice his flesh,Before this earthy prison of their bones;That so the shadows be not unappeased,Nor we disturb'd with prodigies on earth.

TITUS ANDRONICUS

I give him you, the noblest that survives,
The eldest son of this distressed queen.

TAMORA

Stay, Roman brethren! Gracious conqueror,
Victorious Titus, rue the tears I shed,A mother's tears in passion for her son:And if thy sons were ever dear to thee,O, think my son to be as dear to me!Sufficeth not that we are brought to Rome,To beautify thy triumphs and return,Captive to thee and to thy Roman yoke,But must my sons be slaughter'd in the streets,For valiant doings in their country's cause?O, if to

fight for king and commonwealWere piety in thine, it is in these.Andronicus, stain not thy tomb with blood:Wilt thou draw near the nature of the gods?Draw near them then in being merciful:Sweet mercy is nobility's true badge:Thrice noble Titus, spare my first-born son.

TITUS ANDRONICUS	Patient yourself, madam, and pardon me. These are their brethren, whom you Goths beheldAlive and dead, and for their brethren slainReligiously they ask a sacrifice:To this your son is mark'd, and die he must,To appease their groaning shadows that are gone.
LUCIUS	Away with him! and make a fire straight; And with our swords, upon a pile of wood,Let's hew his limbs till they be clean consumed.

Exeunt LUCIUS, QUINTUS, MARTIUS, *and* MUTIUS, *with* ALARBUS

TAMORA	O cruel, irreligious piety!
CHIRON	Was ever Scythia half so barbarous?
DEMETRIUS	Oppose not Scythia to ambitious Rome. Alarbus goes to rest; and we surviveTo tremble under Titus' threatening looks. Then, madam, stand resolved, but hope withalThe self-same gods that arm'd the Queen of TroyWith opportunity of sharp revengeUpon the Thracian tyrant in his tent,May favor Tamora, the Queen of Goths--When Goths were Goths and Tamora was queen--To quit the bloody wrongs upon her foes.

Re-enter LUCIUS, QUINTUS, MARTIUS *and* MUTIUS, *with their swords bloody*

LUCIUS	See, lord and father, how we have perform'd Our Roman rites: Alarbus' limbs are

lopp'd,And entrails feed the sacrificing fire,Whose smoke, like incense, doth perfume the sky.Remaineth nought, but to inter our brethren,And with loud 'larums welcome them to Rome.

TITUS ANDRONICUS Let it be so; and let Andronicus
Make this his latest farewell to their souls.

Trumpets sounded, and the coffin laid in the tomb

In peace and honour rest you here, my sons;
Rome's readiest champions, repose you here in rest,Secure from worldly chances and mishaps!Here lurks no treason, here no envy swells,Here grow no damned grudges; here are no storms,No noise, but silence and eternal sleep:In peace and honour rest you here, my sons!

Enter LAVINIA

LAVINIA In peace and honour live Lord Titus long;
My noble lord and father, live in fame!Lo, at this tomb my tributary tearsI render, for my brethren's obsequies;And at thy feet I kneel, with tears of joy,Shed on the earth, for thy return to Rome:O, bless me here with thy victorious hand,Whose fortunes Rome's best citizens applaud!

TITUS ANDRONICUS Kind Rome, that hast thus lovingly reserved
The cordial of mine age to glad my heart!Lavinia, live; outlive thy father's days,And fame's eternal date, for virtue's praise!

Enter, below, MARCUS ANDRONICUS *and Tribunes; re-enter* SATURNINUS *and* BASSIANUS, *attended*

MARCUS ANDRONICUS Long live Lord Titus, my beloved brother,
Gracious triumpher in the eyes of Rome!

TITUS ANDRONICUS	Thanks, gentle tribune, noble brother Marcus.
MARCUS ANDRONICUS	And welcome, nephews, from successful wars, You that survive, and you that sleep in fame!Fair lords, your fortunes are alike in all,That in your country's service drew your swords:But safer triumph is this funeral pomp,That hath aspired to Solon's happinessAnd triumphs over chance in honour's bed.Titus Andronicus, the people of Rome,Whose friend in justice thou hast ever been,Send thee by me, their tribune and their trust,This palliament of white and spotless hue;And name thee in election for the empire,With these our late-deceased emperor's sons:Be candidatus then, and put it on,And help to set a head on headless Rome.
TITUS ANDRONICUS	A better head her glorious body fits Than his that shakes for age and feebleness:What should I don this robe, and trouble you?Be chosen with proclamations to-day,To-morrow yield up rule, resign my life,And set abroad new business for you all?Rome, I have been thy soldier forty years,And led my country's strength successfully,And buried one and twenty valiant sons,Knighted in field, slain manfully in arms,In right and service of their noble countryGive me a staff of honour for mine age,But not a sceptre to control the world:Upright he held it, lords, that held it last.
MARCUS ANDRONICUS	Titus, thou shalt obtain and ask the empery.
SATURNINUS	Proud and ambitious tribune, canst thou tell?

TITUS ANDRONICUS	Patience, Prince Saturninus.
SATURNINUS	Romans, do me right: Patricians, draw your swords: and sheathe them notTill Saturninus be Rome's emperor.Andronicus, would thou wert shipp'd to hell,Rather than rob me of the people's hearts!
LUCIUS	Proud Saturnine, interrupter of the good That noble-minded Titus means to thee!
TITUS ANDRONICUS	Content thee, prince; I will restore to thee The people's hearts, and wean them from themselves.
BASSIANUS	Andronicus, I do not flatter thee, But honour thee, and will do till I die:My faction if thou strengthen with thy friends,I will most thankful be; and thanks to menOf noble minds is honourable meed.
TITUS ANDRONICUS	People of Rome, and people's tribunes here, I ask your voices and your suffrages:Will you bestow them friendly on Andronicus?
TRIBUNES	To gratify the good Andronicus, And gratulate his safe return to Rome,The people will accept whom he admits.
TITUS ANDRONICUS	Tribunes, I thank you: and this suit I make, That you create your emperor's eldest son,Lord Saturnine; whose virtues will, I hope,Reflect on Rome as Titan's rays on earth,And ripen justice in this commonweal:Then, if you will elect by my advice,Crown him and say 'Long live our emperor!'
MARCUS ANDRONICUS	With voices and applause of every sort, Patricians and plebeians, we createLord Saturninus Rome's great emperor,And say 'Long live our Emperor Saturnine!'

A long flourish till they come down

SATURNINUS Titus Andronicus, for thy favors done To us in our election this day,I give thee thanks in part of thy deserts,And will with deeds requite thy gentleness:And, for an onset, Titus, to advanceThy name and honourable family,Lavinia will I make my empress,Rome's royal mistress, mistress of my heart,And in the sacred Pantheon her espouse:Tell me, Andronicus, doth this motion please thee?

TITUS ANDRONICUS It doth, my worthy lord; and in this match I hold me highly honour'd of your grace:And here in sight of Rome to Saturnine,King and commander of our commonweal,The wide world's emperor, do I consecrateMy sword, my chariot and my prisoners;Presents well worthy Rome's imperial lord:Receive them then, the tribute that I owe,Mine honour's ensigns humbled at thy feet.

SATURNINUS Thanks, noble Titus, father of my life! How proud I am of thee and of thy giftsRome shall record, and when I do forgetThe least of these unspeakable deserts,Romans, forget your fealty to me.

TITUS ANDRONICUS [To TAMORA] Now, madam, are you prisoner to
an emperor;To him that, for your honour and your state,Will use you nobly and your followers.

SATURNINUS A goodly lady, trust me; of the hue That I would choose, were I to choose anew.Clear up, fair queen, that cloudy countenance:Though chance of war hath wrought this change of cheer,Thou comest not to be made a scorn in Rome:Princely shall be thy usage every way.Rest on my

	word, and let not discontentDaunt all your hopes: madam, he comforts youCan make you greater than the Queen of Goths. Lavinia, you are not displeased with this?
LAVINIA	Not I, my lord; sith true nobility Warrants these words in princely courtesy.
SATURNINUS	Thanks, sweet Lavinia. Romans, let us go; Ransomless here we set our prisoners free:Proclaim our honours, lords, with trump and drum.

Flourish. SATURNINUS *courts* TAMORA *in dumb show*

BASSIANUS	Lord Titus, by your leave, this maid is mine.

Seizing LAVINIA

TITUS ANDRONICUS	How, sir! are you in earnest then, my lord?
BASSIANUS	Ay, noble Titus; and resolved withal To do myself this reason and this right.
MARCUS ANDRONICUS	'Suum cuique' is our Roman justice: This prince in justice seizeth but his own.
LUCIUS	And that he will, and shall, if Lucius live.
TITUS ANDRONICUS	Traitors, avaunt! Where is the emperor's guard? Treason, my lord! Lavinia is surprised!
SATURNINUS	Surprised! by whom?
BASSIANUS	By him that justly may Bear his betroth'd from all the world away.

Exeunt BASSIANUS *and* MARCUS *with* LAVINIA

MUTIUS	Brothers, help to convey her hence away, And with my sword I'll keep this door safe.

Exeunt LUCIUS, QUINTUS, *and* MARTIUS

TITUS ANDRONICUS	Follow, my lord, and I'll soon bring her back.
MUTIUS	My lord, you pass not here.
TITUS ANDRONICUS	What, villain boy! Barr'st me my way in Rome?

Stabbing MUTIUS

MUTIUS Help, Lucius, help!

Dies

During the fray, SATURNINUS, TAMORA, DEMETRIUS, CHIRON *and* AARON *go out and re-enter, above*

Re-enter LUCIUS

LUCIUS My lord, you are unjust, and, more than so,
In wrongful quarrel you have slain your son.

TITUS ANDRONICUS Nor thou, nor he, are any sons of mine;
My sons would never so dishonour me:Traitor, restore Lavinia to the emperor.

LUCIUS Dead, if you will; but not to be his wife,
That is another's lawful promised love.

Exit

SATURNINUS No, Titus, no; the emperor needs her not,
Nor her, nor thee, nor any of thy stock:I'll trust, by leisure, him that mocks me once;Thee never, nor thy traitorous haughty sons,Confederates all thus to dishonour me.Was there none else in Rome to make a stale,But Saturnine? Full well, Andronicus,Agree these deeds with that proud brag of thine,That said'st I begg'd the empire at thy hands.

TITUS ANDRONICUS O monstrous! what reproachful words are these?

SATURNINUS But go thy ways; go, give that changing piece
To him that flourish'd for her with his swordA valiant son-in-law thou shalt enjoy;One fit to bandy with thy lawless sons,To ruffle in the commonwealth of Rome.

TITUS ANDRONICUS These words are razors to my wounded heart.

SATURNINUS — And therefore, lovely Tamora, queen of Goths,
That like the stately Phoebe 'mongst her nymphsDost overshine the gallant'st dames of Rome,If thou be pleased with this my sudden choice,Behold, I choose thee, Tamora, for my bride,And will create thee empress of Rome,Speak, Queen of Goths, dost thou applaud my choice?And here I swear by all the Roman gods,Sith priest and holy water are so nearAnd tapers burn so bright and every thingIn readiness for Hymenaeus stand,I will not re-salute the streets of Rome,Or climb my palace, till from forth this placeI lead espoused my bride along with me.

TAMORA — And here, in sight of heaven, to Rome I swear,
If Saturnine advance the Queen of Goths,She will a handmaid be to his desires,A loving nurse, a mother to his youth.

SATURNINUS — Ascend, fair queen, Pantheon. Lords, accompany
Your noble emperor and his lovely bride,Sent by the heavens for Prince Saturnine,Whose wisdom hath her fortune conquered:There shall we consummate our spousal rites.

Exeunt all but TITUS

TITUS ANDRONICUS — I am not bid to wait upon this bride.
Titus, when wert thou wont to walk alone,Dishonour'd thus, and challenged of wrongs?

Re-enter MARCUS, LUCIUS, QUINTUS, *and* MARTIUS

MARCUS ANDRONICUS — O Titus, see, O, see what thou hast done!
In a bad quarrel slain a virtuous son.

TITUS ANDRONICUS	No, foolish tribune, no; no son of mine, Nor thou, nor these, confederates in the deedThat hath dishonour'd all our family;Unworthy brother, and unworthy sons!
LUCIUS	But let us give him burial, as becomes; Give Mutius burial with our brethren.
TITUS ANDRONICUS	Traitors, away! he rests not in this tomb: This monument five hundred years hath stood,Which I have sumptuously re-edified:Here none but soldiers and Rome's servitorsRepose in fame; none basely slain in brawls:Bury him where you can; he comes not here.
MARCUS ANDRONICUS	My lord, this is impiety in you: My nephew Mutius' deeds do plead for himHe must be buried with his brethren.
QUINTUS MARTIUS	And shall, or him we will accompany.
TITUS ANDRONICUS	'And shall!' what villain was it that spake that word?
QUINTUS	He that would vouch it in any place but here.
TITUS ANDRONICUS	What, would you bury him in my despite?
MARCUS ANDRONICUS	No, noble Titus, but entreat of thee To pardon Mutius and to bury him.
TITUS ANDRONICUS	Marcus, even thou hast struck upon my crest, And, with these boys, mine honour thou hast wounded:My foes I do repute you every one;So, trouble me no more, but get you gone.
MARTIUS	He is not with himself; let us withdraw.
QUINTUS	Not I, till Mutius' bones be buried.

MARCUS *and the Sons of* TITUS *kneel*

MARCUS ANDRONICUS	Brother, for in that name doth nature plead,--

QUINTUS	Father, and in that name doth nature speak,--
TITUS ANDRONICUS	Speak thou no more, if all the rest will speed.
MARCUS ANDRONICUS	Renowned Titus, more than half my soul,--
LUCIUS	Dear father, soul and substance of us all,--
MARCUS ANDRONICUS	Suffer thy brother Marcus to inter His noble nephew here in virtue's nest,That died in honour and Lavinia's cause.Thou art a Roman; be not barbarous:The Greeks upon advice did bury AjaxThat slew himself; and wise Laertes' sonDid graciously plead for his funerals:Let not young Mutius, then, that was thy joyBe barr'd his entrance here.
TITUS ANDRONICUS	Rise, Marcus, rise. The dismall'st day is this that e'er I saw,To be dishonour'd by my sons in Rome!Well, bury him, and bury me the next.

MUTIUS *is put into the tomb*

LUCIUS	There lie thy bones, sweet Mutius, with thy friends, Till we with trophies do adorn thy tomb.
ALL	[Kneeling] No man shed tears for noble Mutius; He lives in fame that died in virtue's cause.
MARCUS ANDRONICUS	My lord, to step out of these dreary dumps, How comes it that the subtle Queen of GothsIs of a sudden thus advanced in Rome?
TITUS ANDRONICUS	I know not, Marcus; but I know it is, Whether by device or no, the heavens can tell:Is she not then beholding to the manThat brought her for this high good turn so far?Yes, and will nobly him remunerate.

Flourish. Re-enter, from one side, SATURNINUS *attended,* TAMORA, DEMETRIUS, CHIRON *and AARON; from the other,* BASSIANUS, LAVINIA, *and others*

SATURNINUS So, Bassianus, you have play'd your prize:
God give you joy, sir, of your gallant bride!

BASSIANUS And you of yours, my lord! I say no more,
Nor wish no less; and so, I take my leave.

SATURNINUS Traitor, if Rome have law or we have power,
Thou and thy faction shall repent this rape.

BASSIANUS Rape, call you it, my lord, to seize my own, My truth-betrothed love and now my wife?But let the laws of Rome determine all;Meanwhile I am possess'd of that is mine.

SATURNINUS 'Tis good, sir: you are very short with us;
But, if we live, we'll be as sharp with you.

BASSIANUS My lord, what I have done, as best I may, Answer I must and shall do with my life.Only thus much I give your grace to know:By all the duties that I owe to Rome,This noble gentleman, Lord Titus here,Is in opinion and in honour wrong'd;That in the rescue of LaviniaWith his own hand did slay his youngest son,In zeal to you and highly moved to wrathTo be controll'd in that he frankly gave:Receive him, then, to favor, Saturnine,That hath express'd himself in all his deedsA father and a friend to thee and Rome.

TITUS ANDRONICUS Prince Bassianus, leave to plead my deeds: 'Tis thou and those that have dishonour'd me.Rome and the righteous heavens be my judge,How I have loved and honour'd Saturnine!

TAMORA My worthy lord, if ever Tamora
Were gracious in those princely eyes of

thine,Then hear me speak in indifferently for all;And at my suit, sweet, pardon what is past.

SATURNINUS

What, madam! be dishonour'd openly,
And basely put it up without revenge?

TAMORA

Not so, my lord; the gods of Rome forfend I should be author to dishonour you!But on mine honour dare I undertakeFor good Lord Titus' innocence in all;Whose fury not dissembled speaks his griefs:Then, at my suit, look graciously on him;Lose not so noble a friend on vain suppose,Nor with sour looks afflict his gentle heart.

Aside to SATURNINUS

be won at last;
Dissemble all your griefs and discontents:You are but newly planted in your throne;Lest, then, the people, and patricians too,Upon a just survey, take Titus' part,And so supplant you for ingratitude,Which Rome reputes to be a heinous sin,Yield at entreats; and then let me alone:I'll find a day to massacre them allAnd raze their faction and their family,The cruel father and his traitorous sons,To whom I sued for my dear son's life,And make them know what 'tis to let a queenKneel in the streets and beg for grace in vain.

Aloud

Come, come, sweet emperor; come, Andronicus;
Take up this good old man, and cheer the heartThat dies in tempest of thy angry frown.

SATURNINUS

Rise, Titus, rise; my empress hath prevail'd.

TITUS ANDRONICUS	I thank your majesty, and her, my lord: These words, these looks, infuse new life in me.
TAMORA	Titus, I am incorporate in Rome, A Roman now adopted happily,And must advise the emperor for his good.This day all quarrels die, Andronicus;And let it be mine honour, good my lord,That I have reconciled your friends and you.For you, Prince Bassianus, I have pass'dMy word and promise to the emperor,That you will be more mild and tractable.And fear not lords, and you, Lavinia;By my advice, all humbled on your knees,You shall ask pardon of his majesty.
LUCIUS	We do, and vow to heaven and to his highness, That what we did was mildly as we might,Tendering our sister's honour and our own.
MARCUS ANDRONICUS	That, on mine honour, here I do protest.
SATURNINUS	Away, and talk not; trouble us no more.
TAMORA	Nay, nay, sweet emperor, we must all be friends: The tribune and his nephews kneel for grace;I will not be denied: sweet heart, look back.
SATURNINUS	Marcus, for thy sake and thy brother's here, And at my lovely Tamora's entreats,I do remit these young men's heinous faults: Stand up.Lavinia, though you left me like a churl,I found a friend, and sure as death I sworeI would not part a bachelor from the priest.Come, if the emperor's court can feast two brides,You are my guest, Lavinia, and your friends.This day shall be a love-day, Tamora.

TITUS ANDRONICUS | To-morrow, an it please your majesty To hunt the panther and the hart with me,With horn and hound we'll give your grace bonjour.

SATURNINUS | Be it so, Titus, and gramercy too.

Flourish. Exeunt

ACT-2

SCENE-1 Rome. Before the Palace

Enter AARON

AARON Now climbeth Tamora Olympus' top,
Safe out of fortune's shot; and sits aloft,
Secure of thunder's crack or lightning flash;
Advanced above pale envy's threatening reach.
As when the golden sun salutes the morn,
And, having gilt the ocean with his beams,
Gallops the zodiac in his glistering coach,
And overlooks the highest-peering hills;
So Tamora:
Upon her wit doth earthly honour wait,
And virtue stoops and trembles at her frown.
Then, Aaron, arm thy heart, and fit thy thoughts,
To mount aloft with thy imperial mistress,
And mount her pitch, whom thou in triumph long
Hast prisoner held, fetter'd in amorous chains
And faster bound to Aaron's charming eyes
Than is Prometheus tied to Caucasus.
Away with slavish weeds and servile thoughts!
I will be bright, and shine in pearl and gold,
To wait upon this new-made empress.
To wait, said I? to wanton with this queen,
This goddess, this Semiramis, this nymph,
This siren, that will charm Rome's Saturnine,
And see his shipwreck and his commonweal's.
Holloa! what storm is this?

Enter DEMETRIUS *and* CHIRON, *braving*

DEMETRIUS Chiron, thy years want wit, thy wit wants edge,
And manners, to intrude where I am graced;
And may, for aught thou know'st, affected be.

CHIRON Demetrius, thou dost over-ween in all;
And so in this, to bear me down with braves.
'Tis not the difference of a year or two
Makes me less gracious or thee more fortunate:
I am as able and as fit as thou
To serve, and to deserve my mistress' grace;
And that my sword upon thee shall approve,
And plead my passions for Lavinia's love.

AARON [Aside] Clubs, clubs! these lovers will not keep the peace.

DEMETRIUS Why, boy, although our mother, unadvised,
Gave you a dancing-rapier by your side,
Are you so desperate grown, to threat your friends?
Go to; have your lath glued within your sheath
Till you know better how to handle it.

CHIRON Meanwhile, sir, with the little skill I have,
Full well shalt thou perceive how much I dare.

DEMETRIUS Ay, boy, grow ye so brave?

They draw

AARON [Coming forward] Why, how now, lords!
So near the emperor's palace dare you draw,
And maintain such a quarrel openly?
Full well I wot the ground of all this grudge:
I would not for a million of gold
The cause were known to them it most concerns;
Nor would your noble mother for much more
Be so dishonour'd in the court of Rome.
For shame, put up.

DEMETRIUS Not I, till I have sheathed
My rapier in his bosom and withal

Thrust these reproachful speeches down his throat
That he hath breathed in my dishonour here.

CHIRON For that I am prepared and full resolved.
Foul-spoken coward, that thunder'st with thy tongue,
And with thy weapon nothing darest perform!

AARON Away, I say!
Now, by the gods that warlike Goths adore,
This petty brabble will undo us all.
Why, lords, and think you not how dangerous
It is to jet upon a prince's right?
What, is Lavinia then become so loose,
Or Bassianus so degenerate,
That for her love such quarrels may be broach'd
Without controlment, justice, or revenge?
Young lords, beware! and should the empress know
This discord's ground, the music would not please.

CHIRON I care not, I, knew she and all the world:
I love Lavinia more than all the world.

DEMETRIUS Youngling, learn thou to make some meaner choice:
Lavinia is thine elder brother's hope.

AARON Why, are ye mad? or know ye not, in Rome
How furious and impatient they be,
And cannot brook competitors in love?
I tell you, lords, you do but plot your deaths
By this device.

CHIRON Aaron, a thousand deaths
Would I propose to achieve her whom I love.

AARON To achieve her! how?

DEMETRIUS Why makest thou it so strange?
She is a woman, therefore may be woo'd;
She is a woman, therefore may be won;

She is Lavinia, therefore must be loved.
What, man! more water glideth by the mill
Than wots the miller of; and easy it is
Of a cut loaf to steal a shive, we know:
Though Bassianus be the emperor's brother.
Better than he have worn Vulcan's badge.

AARON
[Aside] Ay, and as good as Saturninus may.

DEMETRIUS
Then why should he despair that knows to court it
With words, fair looks and liberality?
What, hast not thou full often struck a doe,
And borne her cleanly by the keeper's nose?

AARON
Why, then, it seems, some certain snatch or so
Would serve your turns.

CHIRON
Ay, so the turn were served.

DEMETRIUS
Aaron, thou hast hit it.

AARON
Would you had hit it too!
Then should not we be tired with this ado.
Why, hark ye, hark ye! and are you such fools
To square for this? would it offend you, then
That both should speed?

CHIRON
Faith, not me.

DEMETRIUS
Nor me, so I were one.

AARON
For shame, be friends, and join for that you jar:
'Tis policy and stratagem must do
That you affect; and so must you resolve,
That what you cannot as you would achieve,
You must perforce accomplish as you may.
Take this of me: Lucrece was not more chaste
Than this Lavinia, Bassianus' love.
A speedier course than lingering languishment
Must we pursue, and I have found the path.
My lords, a solemn hunting is in hand;
There will the lovely Roman ladies troop:
The forest walks are wide and spacious;
And many unfrequented plots there are
Fitted by kind for rape and villany:

Single you thither then this dainty doe,
And strike her home by force, if not by words:
This way, or not at all, stand you in hope.
Come, come, our empress, with her sacred wit
To villany and vengeance consecrate,
Will we acquaint with all that we intend;
And she shall file our engines with advice,
That will not suffer you to square yourselves,
But to your wishes' height advance you both.
The emperor's court is like the house of Fame,
The palace full of tongues, of eyes, and ears:
The woods are ruthless, dreadful, deaf, and dull;
There speak, and strike, brave boys, and take your turns;
There serve your lusts, shadow'd from heaven's eye,
And revel in Lavinia's treasury.

CHIRON Thy counsel, lad, smells of no cowardice,

DEMETRIUS Sit fas aut nefas, till I find the stream
To cool this heat, a charm to calm these fits.
Per Styga, per manes vehor.

Exeunt

SCENE-2 — A forest near Rome. Horns and cry of hounds heard

Enter Titus Andronicus, *with Hunters, & c.,* Marcus, Lucius, Quintus, *and* Martius

TITUS ANDRONICUS

The hunt is up, the morn is bright and grey,
The fields are fragrant and the woods are green:
Uncouple here and let us make a bay
And wake the emperor and his lovely bride
And rouse the prince and ring a hunter's peal,
That all the court may echo with the noise.
Sons, let it be your charge, as it is ours,
To attend the emperor's person carefully:
I have been troubled in my sleep this night,
But dawning day new comfort hath inspired.

A cry of hounds and horns, winded in a peal. Enter Saturninus, Tamora, Bassianus, Lavinia, Demetrius, Chiron, *and Attendants*

Many good morrows to your majesty;
Madam, to you as many and as good:
I promised your grace a hunter's peal.

SATURNINUS

And you have rung it lustily, my lord;
Somewhat too early for new-married ladies.

BASSIANUS

Lavinia, how say you?

LAVINIA

I say, no;

I have been broad awake two hours and more.

SATURNINUS — Come on, then; horse and chariots let us have,
And to our sport.

To TAMORA

Madam, now shall ye see
Our Roman hunting.

MARCUS ANDRONICUS — I have dogs, my lord,
Will rouse the proudest panther in the chase,
And climb the highest promontory top.

TITUS ANDRONICUS — And I have horse will follow where the game
Makes way, and run like swallows o'er the plain.

DEMETRIUS — Chiron, we hunt not, we, with horse nor hound,
But hope to pluck a dainty doe to ground.

Exeunt

SCENE-3 — A lonely part of the forest

Enter AARON, *with a bag of gold*

AARON He that had wit would think that I had none,
To bury so much gold under a tree,
And never after to inherit it.
Let him that thinks of me so abjectly
Know that this gold must coin a stratagem,
Which, cunningly effected, will beget
A very excellent piece of villany:
And so repose, sweet gold, for their unrest

Hides the gold

That have their alms out of the empress' chest.

Enter TAMORA

TAMORA My lovely Aaron, wherefore look'st thou sad,
When every thing doth make a gleeful boast?
The birds chant melody on every bush,
The snake lies rolled in the cheerful sun,
The green leaves quiver with the cooling wind
And make a chequer'd shadow on the ground:
Under their sweet shade, Aaron, let us sit,
And, whilst the babbling echo mocks the hounds,
Replying shrilly to the well-tuned horns,
As if a double hunt were heard at once,
Let us sit down and mark their yelping noise;
And, after conflict such as was supposed
The wandering prince and Dido once enjoy'd,
When with a happy storm they were surprised
And curtain'd with a counsel-keeping cave,
We may, each wreathed in the other's arms,

Our pastimes done, possess a golden slumber;
Whiles hounds and horns and sweet melodious birds
Be unto us as is a nurse's song
Of lullaby to bring her babe asleep.

AARON Madam, though Venus govern your desires,
Saturn is dominator over mine:
What signifies my deadly-standing eye,
My silence and my cloudy melancholy,
My fleece of woolly hair that now uncurls
Even as an adder when she doth unroll
To do some fatal execution?
No, madam, these are no venereal signs:
Vengeance is in my heart, death in my hand,
Blood and revenge are hammering in my head.
Hark Tamora, the empress of my soul,
Which never hopes more heaven than rests in thee,
This is the day of doom for Bassianus:
His Philomel must lose her tongue to-day,
Thy sons make pillage of her chastity
And wash their hands in Bassianus' blood.
Seest thou this letter? take it up, I pray thee,
And give the king this fatal plotted scroll.
Now question me no more; we are espied;
Here comes a parcel of our hopeful booty,
Which dreads not yet their lives' destruction.

TAMORA Ah, my sweet Moor, sweeter to me than life!

AARON No more, great empress; Bassianus comes:
Be cross with him; and I'll go fetch thy sons
To back thy quarrels, whatsoe'er they be.

Exit

Enter BASSIANUS *and* LAVINIA

BASSIANUS Who have we here? Rome's royal empress,
Unfurnish'd of her well-beseeming troop?
Or is it Dian, habited like her,
Who hath abandoned her holy groves
To see the general hunting in this forest?

TAMORA Saucy controller of our private steps!
Had I the power that some say Dian had,

Thy temples should be planted presently
With horns, as was Actaeon's; and the hounds
Should drive upon thy new-transformed limbs,
Unmannerly intruder as thou art!

LAVINIA Under your patience, gentle empress,
'Tis thought you have a goodly gift in horning;
And to be doubted that your Moor and you
Are singled forth to try experiments:
Jove shield your husband from his hounds to-day!
'Tis pity they should take him for a stag.

BASSIANUS Believe me, queen, your swarth Cimmerian
Doth make your honour of his body's hue,
Spotted, detested, and abominable.
Why are you sequester'd from all your train,
Dismounted from your snow-white goodly steed.
And wander'd hither to an obscure plot,
Accompanied but with a barbarous Moor,
If foul desire had not conducted you?

LAVINIA And, being intercepted in your sport,
Great reason that my noble lord be rated
For sauciness. I pray you, let us hence,
And let her joy her raven-colour'd love;
This valley fits the purpose passing well.

BASSIANUS The king my brother shall have note of this.

LAVINIA Ay, for these slips have made him noted long:
Good king, to be so mightily abused!

TAMORA Why have I patience to endure all this?

Enter DEMETRIUS *and* CHIRON

DEMETRIUS How now, dear sovereign, and our gracious mother!
Why doth your highness look so pale and wan?

TAMORA Have I not reason, think you, to look pale?
These two have 'ticed me hither to this place:
A barren detested vale, you see it is;
The trees, though summer, yet forlorn and lean,
O'ercome with moss and baleful mistletoe:
Here never shines the sun; here nothing breeds,
Unless the nightly owl or fatal raven:

And when they show'd me this abhorred pit,
They told me, here, at dead time of the night,
A thousand fiends, a thousand hissing snakes,
Ten thousand swelling toads, as many urchins,
Would make such fearful and confused cries
As any mortal body hearing it
Should straight fall mad, or else die suddenly.
No sooner had they told this hellish tale,
But straight they told me they would bind me here
Unto the body of a dismal yew,
And leave me to this miserable death:
And then they call'd me foul adulteress,
Lascivious Goth, and all the bitterest terms
That ever ear did hear to such effect:
And, had you not by wondrous fortune come,
This vengeance on me had they executed.
Revenge it, as you love your mother's life,
Or be ye not henceforth call'd my children.

DEMETRIUS This is a witness that I am thy son.

Stabs BASSIANUS

CHIRON And this for me, struck home to show my strength.

Also stabs BASSIANUS, *who dies*

LAVINIA Ay, come, Semiramis, nay, barbarous Tamora,
For no name fits thy nature but thy own!

TAMORA Give me thy poniard; you shall know, my boys
Your mother's hand shall right your mother's wrong.

DEMETRIUS Stay, madam; here is more belongs to her;
First thrash the corn, then after burn the straw:
This minion stood upon her chastity,
Upon her nuptial vow, her loyalty,
And with that painted hope braves your mightiness:
And shall she carry this unto her grave?

CHIRON An if she do, I would I were an eunuch.
Drag hence her husband to some secret hole,
And make his dead trunk pillow to our lust.

TAMORA But when ye have the honey ye desire,
Let not this wasp outlive, us both to sting.

CHIRON — I warrant you, madam, we wil l make that sure.
Come, mistress, now perforce we will enjoy
That nice-preserved honesty of yours.

LAVINIA — O Tamora! thou bear'st a woman's face,--

TAMORA — I will not hear her speak; away with her!

LAVINIA — Sweet lords, entreat her hear me but a word.

DEMETRIUS — Listen, fair madam: let it be your glory
To see her tears; but be your heart to them
As unrelenting flint to drops of rain.

LAVINIA — When did the tiger's young ones teach the dam?
O, do not learn her wrath; she taught it thee;
The milk thou suck'dst from her did turn to marble;
Even at thy teat thou hadst thy tyranny.
Yet every mother breeds not sons alike:

To CHIRON

Do thou entreat her show a woman pity.

CHIRON — What, wouldst thou have me prove myself a bastard?

LAVINIA — 'Tis true; the raven doth not hatch a lark:
Yet have I heard,--O, could I find it now!--
The lion moved with pity did endure
To have his princely paws pared all away:
Some say that ravens foster forlorn children,
The whilst their own birds famish in their nests:
O, be to me, though thy hard heart say no,
Nothing so kind, but something pitiful!

TAMORA — I know not what it means; away with her!

LAVINIA — O, let me teach thee! for my father's sake,
That gave thee life, when well he might have
slain thee,
Be not obdurate, open thy deaf ears.

TAMORA — Hadst thou in person ne'er offended me,
Even for his sake am I pitiless.
Remember, boys, I pour'd forth tears in vain,
To save your brother from the sacrifice;
But fierce Andronicus would not relent;
Therefore, away with her, and use her as you will,
The worse to her, the better loved of me.

LAVINIA O Tamora, be call'd a gentle queen,
And with thine own hands kill me in this place!
For 'tis not life that I have begg'd so long;
Poor I was slain when Bassianus died.

TAMORA What begg'st thou, then? fond woman, let me go.

LAVINIA 'Tis present death I beg; and one thing more
That womanhood denies my tongue to tell:
O, keep me from their worse than killing lust,
And tumble me into some loathsome pit,
Where never man's eye may behold my body:
Do this, and be a charitable murderer.

TAMORA So should I rob my sweet sons of their fee:
No, let them satisfy their lust on thee.

DEMETRIUS Away! for thou hast stay'd us here too long.

LAVINIA No grace? no womanhood? Ah, beastly creature!
The blot and enemy to our general name!
Confusion fall--

CHIRON Nay, then I'll stop your mouth. Bring thou her husband:
This is the hole where Aaron bid us hide him.

DEMETRIUS *throws the body of* BASSIANUS *into the pit; then exeunt* DEMETRIUS *and* CHIRON, *dragging off* LAVINIA

TAMORA Farewell, my sons: see that you make her sure.
Ne'er let my heart know merry cheer indeed,
Till all the Andronici be made away.
Now will I hence to seek my lovely Moor,
And let my spleenful sons this trull deflow'r.

Exit

Re-enter AARON, *with* QUINTUS *and* MARTIUS

AARON Come on, my lords, the better foot before:
Straight will I bring you to the loathsome pit
Where I espied the panther fast asleep.

QUINTUS My sight is very dull, whate'er it bodes.

MARTIUS And mine, I promise you; were't not for shame,
Well could I leave our sport to sleep awhile.

Falls into the pit

QUINTUS — What art thou fall'n? What subtle hole is this,
Whose mouth is cover'd with rude-growing briers,
Upon whose leaves are drops of new-shed blood
As fresh as morning dew distill'd on flowers?
A very fatal place it seems to me.
Speak, brother, hast thou hurt thee with the fall?

MARTIUS — O brother, with the dismall'st object hurt
That ever eye with sight made heart lament!

AARON — [Aside] Now will I fetch the king to find them here,
That he thereby may give a likely guess
How these were they that made away his brother.

Exit

MARTIUS — Why dost not comfort me, and help me out
From this unhallowed and blood-stained hole?

QUINTUS — I am surprised with an uncouth fear;
A chilling sweat o'er-runs my trembling joints:
My heart suspects more than mine eye can see.

MARTIUS — To prove thou hast a true-divining heart,
Aaron and thou look down into this den,
And see a fearful sight of blood and death.

QUINTUS — Aaron is gone; and my compassionate heart
Will not permit mine eyes once to behold
The thing whereat it trembles by surmise;
O, tell me how it is; for ne'er till now
Was I a child to fear I know not what.

MARTIUS — Lord Bassianus lies embrewed here,
All on a heap, like to a slaughter'd lamb,
In this detested, dark, blood-drinking pit.

QUINTUS — If it be dark, how dost thou know 'tis he?

MARTIUS — Upon his bloody finger he doth wear
A precious ring, that lightens all the hole,
Which, like a taper in some monument,

Doth shine upon the dead man's earthy cheeks,
And shows the ragged entrails of the pit:
So pale did shine the moon on Pyramus
When he by night lay bathed in maiden blood.
O brother, help me with thy fainting hand--
If fear hath made thee faint, as me it hath--
Out of this fell devouring receptacle,
As hateful as Cocytus' misty mouth.

QUINTUS Reach me thy hand, that I may help thee out;
Or, wanting strength to do thee so much good,
I may be pluck'd into the swallowing womb
Of this deep pit, poor Bassianus' grave.
I have no strength to pluck thee to the brink.

MARTIUS Nor I no strength to climb without thy help.

QUINTUS Thy hand once more; I will not loose again,
Till thou art here aloft, or I below:
Thou canst not come to me: I come to thee.

Falls in

Enter SATURNINUS *with* AARON

SATURNINUS Along with me: I'll see what hole is here,
And what he is that now is leap'd into it.
Say who art thou that lately didst descend
Into this gaping hollow of the earth?

MARTIUS The unhappy son of old Andronicus:
Brought hither in a most unlucky hour,
To find thy brother Bassianus dead.

SATURNINUS My brother dead! I know thou dost but jest:
He and his lady both are at the lodge
Upon the north side of this pleasant chase;
'Tis not an hour since I left him there.

MARTIUS We know not where you left him all alive;
But, out, alas! here have we found him dead.

Re-enter TAMORA, *with Attendants;* TITUS ANDRONICUS, *and Lucius*

TAMORA Where is my lord the king?

SATURNINUS Here, Tamora, though grieved with killing grief.

TAMORA — Where is thy brother Bassianus?

SATURNINUS — Now to the bottom dost thou search my wound:
Poor Bassianus here lies murdered.

TAMORA — Then all too late I bring this fatal writ,
The complot of this timeless tragedy;
And wonder greatly that man's face can fold
In pleasing smiles such murderous tyranny.

She giveth SATURNINUS *a letter*

SATURNINUS — [Reads] 'An if we miss to meet him handsomely--
Sweet huntsman, Bassianus 'tis we mean--
Do thou so much as dig the grave for him:
Thou know'st our meaning. Look for thy reward
Among the nettles at the elder-tree
Which overshades the mouth of that same pit
Where we decreed to bury Bassianus.
Do this, and purchase us thy lasting friends.'
O Tamora! was ever heard the like?
This is the pit, and this the elder-tree.
Look, sirs, if you can find the huntsman out
That should have murdered Bassianus here.

AARON — My gracious lord, here is the bag of gold.

SATURNINUS — [To TITUS] Two of thy whelps, fell curs of bloody kind,
Have here bereft my brother of his life.
Sirs, drag them from the pit unto the prison:
There let them bide until we have devised
Some never-heard-of torturing pain for them.

TAMORA	What, are they in this pit? O wondrous thing! How easily murder is discovered!
TITUS ANDRONICUS	High emperor, upon my feeble knee I beg this boon, with tears not lightly shed, That this fell fault of my accursed sons, Accursed if the fault be proved in them,--
SATURNINUS	If it be proved! you see it is apparent. Who found this letter? Tamora, was it you?
TAMORA	Andronicus himself did take it up.
TITUS ANDRONICUS	I did, my lord: yet let me be their bail; For, by my father's reverend tomb, I vow They shall be ready at your highness' will To answer their suspicion with their lives.
SATURNINUS	Thou shalt not bail them: see thou follow me. Some bring the murder'd body, some the murderers: Let them not speak a word; the guilt is plain; For, by my soul, were there worse end than death, That end upon them should be executed.
TAMORA	Andronicus, I will entreat the king; Fear not thy sons; they shall do well enough.
TITUS ANDRONICUS	Come, Lucius, come; stay not to talk with them.

Exeunt

SCENE-4 — Another part of the forest

Enter DEMETRIUS *and* CHIRON *with* LAVINIA, *ravished; her hands cut off, and her tongue cut out*

DEMETRIUS So, now go tell, an if thy tongue can speak,
Who 'twas that cut thy tongue and ravish'd thee.

CHIRON Write down thy mind, bewray thy meaning so,
An if thy stumps will let thee play the scribe.

DEMETRIUS See, how with signs and tokens she can scrowl.

CHIRON Go home, call for sweet water, wash thy hands.

DEMETRIUS She hath no tongue to call, nor hands to wash;
And so let's leave her to her silent walks.

CHIRON An 'twere my case, I should go hang myself.

DEMETRIUS If thou hadst hands to help thee knit the cord.

Exeunt DEMETRIUS *and* CHIRON

Enter MARCUS

MARCUS Who is this? my niece, that flies away so fast!
Cousin, a word; where is your husband?
If I do dream, would all my wealth would wake me!
If I do wake, some planet strike me down,
That I may slumber in eternal sleep!
Speak, gentle niece, what stern ungentle hands
Have lopp'd and hew'd and made thy body bare
Of her two branches, those sweet ornaments,
Whose circling shadows kings have sought to sleep in,

And might not gain so great a happiness
As have thy love? Why dost not speak to me? Alas, a crimson river of warm blood,
Like to a bubbling fountain stirr'd with wind,
Doth rise and fall between thy rosed lips,
Coming and going with thy honey breath.
But, sure, some Tereus hath deflowered thee,
And, lest thou shouldst detect him, cut thy tongue.
Ah, now thou turn'st away thy face for shame!
And, notwithstanding all this loss of blood,
As from a conduit with three issuing spouts,
Yet do thy cheeks look red as Titan's face
Blushing to be encountered with a cloud.
Shall I speak for thee? shall I say 'tis so?
O, that I knew thy heart; and knew the beast,
That I might rail at him, to ease my mind!
Sorrow concealed, like an oven stopp'd,
Doth burn the heart to cinders where it is.
Fair Philomela, she but lost her tongue,
And in a tedious sampler sew'd her mind:
But, lovely niece, that mean is cut from thee;
A craftier Tereus, cousin, hast thou met,
And he hath cut those pretty fingers off,
That could have better sew'd than Philomel.
O, had the monster seen those lily hands
Tremble, like aspen-leaves, upon a lute,
And make the silken strings delight to kiss them,
He would not then have touch'd them for his life!
Or, had he heard the heavenly harmony
Which that sweet tongue hath made,
He would have dropp'd his knife, and fell asleep
As Cerberus at the Thracian poet's feet.
Come, let us go, and make thy father blind;
For such a sight will blind a father's eye:
One hour's storm will drown the fragrant meads;
What will whole months of tears thy father's eyes?
Do not draw back, for we will mourn with thee
O, could our mourning ease thy misery!

Exeunt

ACT-3

SCENE-1— Rome. A street

Enter Judges, Senators and Tribunes, with MARTIUS *and* QUINTUS, *bound, passing on to the place of execution;* TITUS *going before, pleading*

TITUS ANDRONICUS

Hear me, grave fathers! noble tribunes, stay!
For pity of mine age, whose youth was spent
In dangerous wars, whilst you securely slept;
For all my blood in Rome's great quarrel shed;
For all the frosty nights that I have watch'd;
And for these bitter tears, which now you see
Filling the aged wrinkles in my cheeks;
Be pitiful to my condemned sons,
Whose souls are not corrupted as 'tis thought.
For two and twenty sons I never wept,
Because they died in honour's lofty bed.

Lieth down; the Judges, & c., pass by him, and Exeunt

For these, these, tribunes, in the dust I write
My heart's deep languor and my soul's sad tears:
Let my tears stanch the earth's dry appetite;
My sons' sweet blood will make it shame and blush.

O earth, I will befriend thee more with rain,
That shall distil from these two ancient urns,
Than youthful April shall with all his showers:
In summer's drought I'll drop upon thee still;
In winter with warm tears I'll melt the snow
And keep eternal spring-time on thy face,
So thou refuse to drink my dear sons' blood.

Enter LUCIUS, *with his sword drawn*

O reverend tribunes! O gentle, aged men!
Unbind my sons, reverse the doom of death;
And let me say, that never wept before,
My tears are now prevailing orators.

LUCIUS

O noble father, you lament in vain:
The tribunes hear you not; no man is by;
And you recount your sorrows to a stone.

TITUS ANDRONICUS

Ah, Lucius, for thy brothers let me plead.
Grave tribunes, once more I entreat of you,--

LUCIUS

My gracious lord, no tribune hears you speak.

TITUS ANDRONICUS

Why, tis no matter, man; if they did hear,
They would not mark me, or if they did mark,
They would not pity me, yet plead I must;
Therefore I tell my sorrows to the stones;
Who, though they cannot answer my distress,
Yet in some sort they are better than the tribunes,
For that they will not intercept my tale:
When I do weep, they humbly at my feet

Receive my tears and seem to weep with me;
And, were they but attired in grave weeds,
Rome could afford no tribune like to these.
A stone is soft as wax,--tribunes more hard than stones;
A stone is silent, and offendeth not,
And tribunes with their tongues doom men to death.

Rises

But wherefore stand'st thou with thy weapon drawn?

LUCIUS	To rescue my two brothers from their death: For which attempt the judges have pronounced My everlasting doom of banishment.
TITUS ANDRONICUS	O happy man! they have befriended thee. Why, foolish Lucius, dost thou not perceive That Rome is but a wilderness of tigers? Tigers must prey, and Rome affords no prey But me and mine: how happy art thou, then, From these devourers to be banished! But who comes with our brother Marcus here?

Enter MARCUS *and* LAVINIA

MARCUS ANDRONICUS	Titus, prepare thy aged eyes to weep; Or, if not so, thy noble heart to break: I bring consuming sorrow to thine age.
TITUS ANDRONICUS	Will it consume me? let me see it, then.
MARCUS ANDRONICUS	This was thy daughter.
TITUS ANDRONICUS	Why, Marcus, so she is.
LUCIUS	Ay me, this object kills me!
TITUS ANDRONICUS	Faint-hearted boy, arise, and look upon her.

Speak, Lavinia, what accursed hand
Hath made thee handless in thy father's sight?
What fool hath added water to the sea,
Or brought a faggot to bright-burning Troy?
My grief was at the height before thou camest,
And now like Nilus, it disdaineth bounds.
Give me a sword, I'll chop off my hands too;
For they have fought for Rome, and all in vain;
And they have nursed this woe, in feeding life;
In bootless prayer have they been held up,
And they have served me to effectless use:
Now all the service I require of them
Is that the one will help to cut the other.
'Tis well, Lavinia, that thou hast no hands;
For hands, to do Rome service, are but vain.

LUCIUS — Speak, gentle sister, who hath martyr'd thee?

MARCUS ANDRONICUS — O, that delightful engine of her thoughts
That blabb'd them with such pleasing eloquence,
Is torn from forth that pretty hollow cage,
Where, like a sweet melodious bird, it sung
Sweet varied notes, enchanting every ear!

LUCIUS — O, say thou for her, who hath done this deed?

MARCUS ANDRONICUS — O, thus I found her, straying in the park,
Seeking to hide herself, as doth the deer
That hath received some unrecuring wound.

TITUS ANDRONICUS — It was my deer; and he that wounded her
Hath hurt me more than had he killed me dead:

For now I stand as one upon a rock
Environed with a wilderness of sea,
Who marks the waxing tide grow wave by wave,
Expecting ever when some envious surge
Will in his brinish bowels swallow him.
This way to death my wretched sons are gone;
Here stands my other son, a banished man,
And here my brother, weeping at my woes.
But that which gives my soul the greatest spurn,
Is dear Lavinia, dearer than my soul.
Had I but seen thy picture in this plight,
It would have madded me: what shall I do
Now I behold thy lively body so?
Thou hast no hands, to wipe away thy tears:
Nor tongue, to tell me who hath martyr'd thee:
Thy husband he is dead: and for his death
Thy brothers are condemn'd, and dead by this.
Look, Marcus! ah, son Lucius, look on her!
When I did name her brothers, then fresh tears
Stood on her cheeks, as doth the honey-dew
Upon a gather'd lily almost wither'd.

MARCUS ANDRONICUS
Perchance she weeps because they kill'd her husband;
Perchance because she knows them innocent.

TITUS ANDRONICUS
If they did kill thy husband, then be joyful
Because the law hath ta'en revenge on them.
No, no, they would not do so foul a deed;
Witness the sorrow that their sister makes.

Gentle Lavinia, let me kiss thy lips.
Or make some sign how I may do thee ease:
Shall thy good uncle, and thy brother Lucius,
And thou, and I, sit round about some fountain,
Looking all downwards to behold our cheeks
How they are stain'd, as meadows, yet not dry,
With miry slime left on them by a flood?
And in the fountain shall we gaze so long
Till the fresh taste be taken from that clearness,
And made a brine-pit with our bitter tears?
Or shall we cut away our hands, like thine?
Or shall we bite our tongues, and in dumb shows
Pass the remainder of our hateful days?
What shall we do? let us, that have our tongues,
Plot some deuce of further misery,
To make us wonder'd at in time to come.

LUCIUS
Sweet father, cease your tears; for, at your grief,
See how my wretched sister sobs and weeps.

MARCUS ANDRONICUS
Patience, dear niece. Good Titus, dry thine eyes.

TITUS ANDRONICUS
Ah, Marcus, Marcus! brother, well I wot
Thy napkin cannot drink a tear of mine,
For thou, poor man, hast drown'd it with thine own.

LUCIUS
Ah, my Lavinia, I will wipe thy cheeks.

TITUS ANDRONICUS
Mark, Marcus, mark! I understand her signs:
Had she a tongue to speak, now would she say

That to her brother which I said to thee:
His napkin, with his true tears all bewet,
Can do no service on her sorrowful cheeks.
O, what a sympathy of woe is this,
As far from help as Limbo is from bliss!

Enter AARON

AARON

Titus Andronicus, my lord the emperor
Sends thee this word,--that, if thou love thy sons,
Let Marcus, Lucius, or thyself, old Titus,
Or any one of you, chop off your hand,
And send it to the king: he for the same
Will send thee hither both thy sons alive;
And that shall be the ransom for their fault.

TITUS ANDRONICUS

O gracious emperor! O gentle Aaron!
Did ever raven sing so like a lark,
That gives sweet tidings of the sun's uprise?
With all my heart, I'll send the emperor
My hand:
Good Aaron, wilt thou help to chop it off?

LUCIUS

Stay, father! for that noble hand of thine,
That hath thrown down so many enemies,
Shall not be sent: my hand will serve the turn:
My youth can better spare my blood than you;
And therefore mine shall save my brothers' lives.

MARCUS ANDRONICUS

Which of your hands hath not defended Rome,
And rear'd aloft the bloody battle-axe,
Writing destruction on the enemy's castle?
O, none of both but are of high desert:
My hand hath been but idle; let it serve
To ransom my two nephews from their death;

Then have I kept it to a worthy end.

AARON — Nay, come, agree whose hand shall go along,
For fear they die before their pardon come.

MARCUS ANDRONICUS — My hand shall go.

LUCIUS — By heaven, it shall not go!

TITUS ANDRONICUS — Sirs, strive no more: such wither'd herbs as these
Are meet for plucking up, and therefore mine.

LUCIUS — Sweet father, if I shall be thought thy son,
Let me redeem my brothers both from death.

MARCUS ANDRONICUS — And, for our father's sake and mother's care,
Now let me show a brother's love to thee.

TITUS ANDRONICUS — Agree between you; I will spare my hand.

LUCIUS — Then I'll go fetch an axe.

MARCUS ANDRONICUS — But I will use the axe.

Exeunt LUCIUS *and* MARCUS

TITUS ANDRONICUS — Come hither, Aaron; I'll deceive them both:
Lend me thy hand, and I will give thee mine.

AARON — [Aside] If that be call'd deceit, I will be honest,
And never, whilst I live, deceive men so:
But I'll deceive you in another sort,
And that you'll say, ere half an hour pass.

Cuts off TITUS'S *hand*

Re-enter LUCIUS *and* MARCUS

TITUS ANDRONICUS — Now stay your strife: what shall be is dispatch'd.
Good Aaron, give his majesty my hand:
Tell him it was a hand that warded him
From thousand dangers; bid him bury it

More hath it merited; that let it have.
As for my sons, say I account of them
As jewels purchased at an easy price;
And yet dear too, because I bought mine own.

AARON
I go, Andronicus: and for thy hand
Look by and by to have thy sons with thee.

Aside

Their heads, I mean. O, how this villany
Doth fat me with the very thoughts of it!
Let fools do good, and fair men call for grace.
Aaron will have his soul black like his face.

Exit

TITUS ANDRONICUS
O, here I lift this one hand up to heaven,
And bow this feeble ruin to the earth:
If any power pities wretched tears,
To that I call!

To LAVINIA

What, wilt thou kneel with me?
Do, then, dear heart; for heaven shall hear our prayers;
Or with our sighs we'll breathe the welkin dim,
And stain the sun with fog, as sometime clouds
When they do hug him in their melting bosoms.

MARCUS ANDRONICUS
O brother, speak with possibilities,
And do not break into these deep extremes.

TITUS ANDRONICUS
Is not my sorrow deep, having no bottom?
Then be my passions bottomless with them.

MARCUS ANDRONICUS
But yet let reason govern thy lament.

TITUS ANDRONICUS If there were reason for these miseries,
Then into limits could I bind my woes:
When heaven doth weep, doth not the earth o'erflow?
If the winds rage, doth not the sea wax mad,
Threatening the welkin with his big-swoln face?
And wilt thou have a reason for this coil?
I am the sea; hark, how her sighs do blow!
She is the weeping welkin, I the earth:
Then must my sea be moved with her sighs;
Then must my earth with her continual tears
Become a deluge, overflow'd and drown'd;
For why my bowels cannot hide her woes,
But like a drunkard must I vomit them.
Then give me leave, for losers will have leave
To ease their stomachs with their bitter tongues.

Enter a Messenger, with two heads and a hand

MESSENGER Worthy Andronicus, ill art thou repaid
For that good hand thou sent'st the emperor.
Here are the heads of thy two noble sons;
And here's thy hand, in scorn to thee sent back;
Thy griefs their sports, thy resolution mock'd;
That woe is me to think upon thy woes
More than remembrance of my father's death.

Exit

MARCUS ANDRONICUS Now let hot AEtna cool in Sicily,
And be my heart an ever-burning hell!

These miseries are more than may be borne.
To weep with them that weep doth ease some deal;
But sorrow flouted at is double death.

LUCIUS

Ah, that this sight should make so deep a wound,
And yet detested life not shrink thereat!
That ever death should let life bear his name,
Where life hath no more interest but to breathe!

LAVINIA *kisses* TITUS

MARCUS ANDRONICUS

Alas, poor heart, that kiss is comfortless
As frozen water to a starved snake.

TITUS ANDRONICUS

When will this fearful slumber have an end?

MARCUS ANDRONICUS

Now, farewell, flattery: die, Andronicus;
Thou dost not slumber: see, thy two sons' heads,
Thy warlike hand, thy mangled daughter here:
Thy other banish'd son, with this dear sight
Struck pale and bloodless; and thy brother, I,
Even like a stony image, cold and numb.
Ah, now no more will I control thy griefs:
Rend off thy silver hair, thy other hand
Gnawing with thy teeth; and be this dismal sight
The closing up of our most wretched eyes;
Now is a time to storm; why art thou still?

TITUS ANDRONICUS

Ha, ha, ha!

MARCUS ANDRONICUS

Why dost thou laugh? it fits not with this hour.

TITUS ANDRONICUS

Why, I have not another tear to shed:
Besides, this sorrow is an enemy,

And would usurp upon my watery eyes
And make them blind with tributary tears:
Then which way shall I find Revenge's cave?
For these two heads do seem to speak to me,
And threat me I shall never come to bliss
Till all these mischiefs be return'd again
Even in their throats that have committed them.
Come, let me see what task I have to do.
You heavy people, circle me about,
That I may turn me to each one of you,
And swear unto my soul to right your wrongs.
The vow is made. Come, brother, take a head;
And in this hand the other I will bear.
Lavinia, thou shalt be employ'd: these arms!
Bear thou my hand, sweet wench, between thy teeth.
As for thee, boy, go get thee from my sight;
Thou art an exile, and thou must not stay:
Hie to the Goths, and raise an army there:
And, if you love me, as I think you do,
Let's kiss and part, for we have much to do.

Exeunt TITUS, MARCUS, *and* LAVINIA

LUCIUS

Farewell Andronicus, my noble father,
The wofull'st man that ever lived in Rome:
Farewell, proud Rome; till Lucius come again,
He leaves his pledges dearer than his life:
Farewell, Lavinia, my noble sister;
O, would thou wert as thou tofore hast been!
But now nor Lucius nor Lavinia lives
But in oblivion and hateful griefs.

If Lucius live, he will requite your wrongs;
And make proud Saturnine and his empress
Beg at the gates, like Tarquin and his queen.
Now will I to the Goths, and raise a power,
To be revenged on Rome and Saturnine.

Exit

SCENE-2 — A room in Titus's house. A banquet set out

Enter TITUS, MARCUS, LAVINIA *and Young* LUCIUS, *a boy*

TITUS ANDRONICUS

So, so; now sit: and look you eat no more
Than will preserve just so much strength in us
As will revenge these bitter woes of ours.
Marcus, unknit that sorrow-wreathen knot:
Thy niece and I, poor creatures, want our hands,
And cannot passionate our tenfold grief
With folded arms. This poor right hand of mine
Is left to tyrannize upon my breast;
Who, when my heart, all mad with misery,
Beats in this hollow prison of my flesh,
Then thus I thump it down.

To LAVINIA

Thou map of woe, that thus dost talk in signs!
When thy poor heart beats with outrageous beating,
Thou canst not strike it thus to make it still.
Wound it with sighing, girl, kill it with groans;
Or get some little knife between thy teeth,
And just against thy heart make thou a hole;

That all the tears that thy poor eyes let fall
May run into that sink, and soaking in
Drown the lamenting fool in sea-salt tears.

MARCUS ANDRONICUS
Fie, brother, fie! teach her not thus to lay
Such violent hands upon her tender life.

TITUS ANDRONICUS
How now! has sorrow made thee dote already?
Why, Marcus, no man should be mad but I.
What violent hands can she lay on her life?
Ah, wherefore dost thou urge the name of hands;
To bid AEneas tell the tale twice o'er,
How Troy was burnt and he made miserable?
O, handle not the theme, to talk of hands,
Lest we remember still that we have none.
Fie, fie, how franticly I square my talk,
As if we should forget we had no hands,
If Marcus did not name the word of hands!
Come, let's fall to; and, gentle girl, eat this:
Here is no drink! Hark, Marcus, what she says;
I can interpret all her martyr'd signs;
She says she drinks no other drink but tears,
Brew'd with her sorrow, mesh'd upon her cheeks:
Speechless complainer, I will learn thy thought;
In thy dumb action will I be as perfect
As begging hermits in their holy prayers:
Thou shalt not sigh, nor hold thy stumps to heaven,
Nor wink, nor nod, nor kneel, nor make a sign,
But I of these will wrest an alphabet
And by still practise learn to know thy meaning.

Young LUCIUS	Good grandsire, leave these bitter deep laments: Make my aunt merry with some pleasing tale.
MARCUS ANDRONICUS	Alas, the tender boy, in passion moved, Doth weep to see his grandsire's heaviness.
TITUS ANDRONICUS	Peace, tender sapling; thou art made of tears, And tears will quickly melt thy life away.

MARCUS *strikes the dish with a knife*

	What dost thou strike at, Marcus, with thy knife?
MARCUS ANDRONICUS	At that that I have kill'd, my lord; a fly.
TITUS ANDRONICUS	Out on thee, murderer! thou kill'st my heart; Mine eyes are cloy'd with view of tyranny: A deed of death done on the innocent Becomes not Titus' brother: get thee gone: I see thou art not for my company.
MARCUS ANDRONICUS	Alas, my lord, I have but kill'd a fly.
TITUS ANDRONICUS	But how, if that fly had a father and mother? How would he hang his slender gilded wings, And buzz lamenting doings in the air! Poor harmless fly, That, with his pretty buzzing melody, Came here to make us merry! and thou hast kill'd him.
MARCUS ANDRONICUS	Pardon me, sir; it was a black ill-favor'd fly, Like to the empress' Moor; therefore I kill'd him.
TITUS ANDRONICUS	O, O, O, Then pardon me for reprehending thee, For thou hast done a charitable deed. Give me thy knife, I will insult on him;

Flattering myself, as if it were the Moor
Come hither purposely to poison me.--
There's for thyself, and that's for Tamora.
Ah, sirrah!
Yet, I think, we are not brought so low,
But that between us we can kill a fly
That comes in likeness of a coal-black Moor.

MARCUS ANDRONICUS Alas, poor man! grief has so wrought on him,
He takes false shadows for true substances.

TITUS ANDRONICUS Come, take away. Lavinia, go with me:
I'll to thy closet; and go read with thee
Sad stories chanced in the times of old.
Come, boy, and go with me: thy sight is young,
And thou shalt read when mine begin to dazzle.

Exeunt

ACT-4

SCENE-1 — Rome. Titus's garden

Enter young LUCIUS, *and* LAVINIA *running after him, and the boy flies from her, with books under his arm. Then enter* TITUS *and* MARCUS

Young LUCIUS	Help, grandsire, help! my aunt Lavinia Follows me every where, I know not why: Good uncle Marcus, see how swift she comes. Alas, sweet aunt, I know not what you mean.
MARCUS ANDRONICUS	Stand by me, Lucius; do not fear thine aunt.
TITUS ANDRONICUS	She loves thee, boy, too well to do thee harm.
Young LUCIUS	Ay, when my father was in Rome she did.
MARCUS ANDRONICUS	What means my niece Lavinia by these signs?
TITUS ANDRONICUS	Fear her not, Lucius: somewhat doth she mean: See, Lucius, see how much she makes of thee: Somewhither would she have thee go with her. Ah, boy, Cornelia never with more care Read to her sons than she hath read to thee Sweet poetry and Tully's Orator.
MARCUS ANDRONICUS	Canst thou not guess wherefore she plies thee thus?

Young LUCIUS — My lord, I know not, I, nor can I guess,
Unless some fit or frenzy do possess her:
For I have heard my grandsire say full oft,
Extremity of griefs would make men mad;
And I have read that Hecuba of Troy
Ran mad through sorrow: that made me to fear;
Although, my lord, I know my noble aunt
Loves me as dear as e'er my mother did,
And would not, but in fury, fright my youth:
Which made me down to throw my books, and fly--
Causeless, perhaps. But pardon me, sweet aunt:
And, madam, if my uncle Marcus go,
I will most willingly attend your ladyship.

MARCUS ANDRONICUS — Lucius, I will.

LAVINIA *turns over with her stumps the books which* LUCIUS *has let fall*

TITUS ANDRONICUS — How now, Lavinia! Marcus, what means this?
Some book there is that she desires to see.
Which is it, girl, of these? Open them, boy.
But thou art deeper read, and better skill'd
Come, and take choice of all my library,
And so beguile thy sorrow, till the heavens
Reveal the damn'd contriver of this deed.
Why lifts she up her arms in sequence thus?

MARCUS ANDRONICUS — I think she means that there was more than one
Confederate in the fact: ay, more there was;
Or else to heaven she heaves them for revenge.

TITUS ANDRONICUS — Lucius, what book is that she tosseth so?

Young LUCIUS — Grandsire, 'tis Ovid's Metamorphoses;
My mother gave it me.

MARCUS ANDRONICUS For love of her that's gone,
Perhaps she cull'd it from among the rest.

TITUS ANDRONICUS Soft! see how busily she turns the leaves!

Helping her

What would she find? Lavinia, shall I read?
This is the tragic tale of Philomel,
And treats of Tereus' treason and his rape:
And rape, I fear, was root of thine annoy.

MARCUS ANDRONICUS See, brother, see; note how she quotes the leaves.

TITUS ANDRONICUS Lavinia, wert thou thus surprised, sweet girl,
Ravish'd and wrong'd, as Philomela was,
Forced in the ruthless, vast, and gloomy woods? See, see!
Ay, such a place there is, where we did hunt--
O, had we never, never hunted there!--
Pattern'd by that the poet here describes,
By nature made for murders and for rapes.

MARCUS ANDRONICUS O, why should nature build so foul a den,
Unless the gods delight in tragedies?

TITUS ANDRONICUS Give signs, sweet girl, for here are none but friends,
What Roman lord it was durst do the deed:
Or slunk not Saturnine, as Tarquin erst,
That left the camp to sin in Lucrece' bed?

MARCUS ANDRONICUS Sit down, sweet niece: brother, sit down by me.
Apollo, Pallas, Jove, or Mercury,
Inspire me, that I may this treason find!
My lord, look here: look here, Lavinia:
This sandy plot is plain; guide, if thou canst
This after me, when I have writ my name
Without the help of any hand at all.

He writes his name with his staff, and guides it with feet and mouth

Cursed be that heart that forced us to this shift!
Write thou good niece; and here display, at last,
What God will have discover'd for revenge;
Heaven guide thy pen to print thy sorrows plain,
That we may know the traitors and the truth!

She takes the staff in her mouth, and guides it with her stumps, and writes

TITUS ANDRONICUS O, do ye read, my lord, what she hath writ?
'Stuprum. Chiron. Demetrius.'

MARCUS ANDRONICUS What, what! the lustful sons of Tamora
Performers of this heinous, bloody deed?

TITUS ANDRONICUS Magni Dominator poli,
Tam lentus audis scelera? tam lentus vides?

MARCUS ANDRONICUS O, calm thee, gentle lord; although I know
There is enough written upon this earth
To stir a mutiny in the mildest thoughts
And arm the minds of infants to exclaims.
My lord, kneel down with me; Lavinia, kneel;
And kneel, sweet boy, the Roman Hector's hope;
And swear with me, as, with the woful fere
And father of that chaste dishonour'd dame,
Lord Junius Brutus sware for Lucrece' rape,
That we will prosecute by good advice
Mortal revenge upon these traitorous Goths,
And see their blood, or die with this reproach.

TITUS ANDRONICUS 'Tis sure enough, an you knew how.
But if you hunt these bear-whelps, then beware:

The dam will wake; and, if she wind you once,
She's with the lion deeply still in league,
And lulls him whilst she playeth on her back,
And when he sleeps will she do what she list.
You are a young huntsman, Marcus; let it alone;
And, come, I will go get a leaf of brass,
And with a gad of steel will write these words,
And lay it by: the angry northern wind
Will blow these sands, like Sibyl's leaves, abroad,
And where's your lesson, then? Boy, what say you?

Young LUCIUS
I say, my lord, that if I were a man,
Their mother's bed-chamber should not be safe
For these bad bondmen to the yoke of Rome.

MARCUS ANDRONICUS
Ay, that's my boy! thy father hath full oft
For his ungrateful country done the like.

Young LUCIUS
And, uncle, so will I, an if I live.

TITUS ANDRONICUS
Come, go with me into mine armoury;
Lucius, I'll fit thee; and withal, my boy,
Shalt carry from me to the empress' sons
Presents that I intend to send them both:
Come, come; thou'lt do thy message, wilt thou not?

Young LUCIUS
Ay, with my dagger in their bosoms, grandsire.

TITUS ANDRONICUS
No, boy, not so; I'll teach thee another course.
Lavinia, come. Marcus, look to my house:
Lucius and I'll go brave it at the court:
Ay, marry, will we, sir; and we'll be waited on.

Exeunt TITUS, LAVINIA, *and Young* LUCIUS

MARCUS ANDRONICUS O heavens, can you hear a good man groan,
And not relent, or not compassion him?
Marcus, attend him in his ecstasy,
That hath more scars of sorrow in his heart
Than foemen's marks upon his batter'd shield;
But yet so just that he will not revenge.
Revenge, ye heavens, for old Andronicus!

Exit

SCENE-2 — The same. A room in the palace

Enter, from one side, AARON, DEMETRIUS, *and* CHIRON; *from the other side, Young* LUCIUS, *and an Attendant, with a bundle of weapons, and verses writ upon them*

CHIRON

Demetrius, here's the son of Lucius;
He hath some message to deliver us.

AARON

Ay, some mad message from his mad grandfather.

Young LUCIUS

My lords, with all the humbleness I may,
I greet your honours from Andronicus.

Aside

And pray the Roman gods confound you both!

DEMETRIUS

Gramercy, lovely Lucius: what's the news?

Young LUCIUS

[Aside] That you are both decipher'd, that's the news,
For villains mark'd with rape.--May it please you,
My grandsire, well advised, hath sent by me
The goodliest weapons of his armoury
To gratify your honourable youth,
The hope of Rome; for so he bade me say;
And so I do, and with his gifts present
Your lordships, that, whenever you have need,
You may be armed and appointed well:
And so I leave you both:

Aside

like bloody villains.

Exeunt Young LUCIUS, *and Attendant*

DEMETRIUS What's here? A scroll; and written round about?
Let's see;

Reads

'Integer vitae, scelerisque purus,
Non eget Mauri jaculis, nec arcu.'

CHIRON O, 'tis a verse in Horace; I know it well:
I read it in the grammar long ago.

AARON Ay, just; a verse in Horace; right, you have it.

Aside

Now, what a thing it is to be an ass!
Here's no sound jest! the old man hath found their guilt;
And sends them weapons wrapped about with lines,
That wound, beyond their feeling, to the quick.
But were our witty empress well afoot,
She would applaud Andronicus' conceit:
But let her rest in her unrest awhile.
And now, young lords, was't not a happy star
Led us to Rome, strangers, and more than so,
Captives, to be advanced to this height?
It did me good, before the palace gate
To brave the tribune in his brother's hearing.

DEMETRIUS But me more good, to see so great a lord
Basely insinuate and send us gifts.

AARON Had he not reason, Lord Demetrius?
Did you not use his daughter very friendly?

DEMETRIUS I would we had a thousand Roman dames
At such a bay, by turn to serve our lust.

CHIRON A charitable wish and full of love.

AARON Here lacks but your mother for to say amen.

CHIRON And that would she for twenty thousand more.

DEMETRIUS Come, let us go; and pray to all the gods
For our beloved mother in her pains.

AARON	[Aside] Pray to the devils; the gods have given us over.

Trumpets sound within

DEMETRIUS	Why do the emperor's trumpets flourish thus?
CHIRON	Belike, for joy the emperor hath a son.
DEMETRIUS	Soft! who comes here?

Enter a Nurse, with a blackamoor Child in her arms

NURSE	Good morr ow, lords: O, tell me, did you see Aaron the Moor?
AARON	Well, more or less, or ne'er a whit at all, Here Aaron is; and what with Aaron now?
NURSE	O gentle Aaron, we are all undone! Now help, or woe betide thee evermore!
AARON	Why, what a caterwauling dost thou keep! What dost thou wrap and fumble in thine arms?
NURSE	O, that which I would hide from heaven's eye, Our empress' shame, and stately Rome's disgrace! She is deliver'd, lords; she is deliver'd.
AARON	To whom?
NURSE	I mean, she is brought a-bed.
AARON	Well, God give her good rest! What hath he sent her?
NURSE	A devil.
AARON	Why, then she is the devil's dam; a joyful issue.
NURSE	A joyless, dismal, black, and sorrowful issue: Here is the babe, as loathsome as a toad Amongst the fairest breeders of our clime: The empress sends it thee, thy stamp, thy seal, And bids thee christen it with thy dagger's point.
AARON	'Zounds, ye whore! is black so base a hue? Sweet blowse, you are a beauteous blossom, sure.

DEMETRIUS Villain, what hast thou done?

AARON That which thou canst not undo.

CHIRON Thou hast undone our mother.

AARON Villain, I have done thy mother.

DEMETRIUS And therein, hellish dog, thou hast undone.
Woe to her chance, and damn'd her loathed choice!
Accursed the offspring of so foul a fiend!

CHIRON It shall not live.

AARON It shall not die.

NURSE Aaron, it must; the mother wills it so.

AARON What, must it, nurse? then let no man but I
Do execution on my flesh and blood.

DEMETRIUS I'll broach the tadpole on my rapier's point:
Nurse, give it me; my sword shall soon dispatch it.

AARON Sooner this sword shall plough thy bowels up.

Takes the Child from the Nurse, and draws

Stay, murderous villains! will you kill your brother?
Now, by the burning tapers of the sky,
That shone so brightly when this boy was got,
He dies upon my scimitar's sharp point
That touches this my first-born son and heir!
I tell you, younglings, not Enceladus,
With all his threatening band of Typhon's brood,
Nor great Alcides, nor the god of war,
Shall seize this prey out of his father's hands.
What, what, ye sanguine, shallow-hearted boys!
Ye white-limed walls! ye alehouse painted signs!
Coal-black is better than another hue,
In that it scorns to bear another hue;
For all the water in the ocean

Can never turn the swan's black legs to white,
Although she lave them hourly in the flood.
Tell the empress from me, I am of age
To keep mine own, excuse it how she can.

DEMETRIUS Wilt thou betray thy noble mistress thus?

AARON My mistress is my mistress; this myself,
The vigour and the picture of my youth:
This before all the world do I prefer;
This maugre all the world will I keep safe,
Or some of you shall smoke for it in Rome.

DEMETRIUS By this our mother is forever shamed.

CHIRON Rome will despise her for this foul escape.

NURSE The emperor, in his rage, will doom her death.

CHIRON I blush to think upon this ignomy.

AARON Why, there's the privilege your beauty bears:
Fie, treacherous hue, that will betray with blushing
The close enacts and counsels of the heart!
Here's a young lad framed of another leer:
Look, how the black slave smiles upon the father,
As who should say 'Old lad, I am thine own.'
He is your brother, lords, sensibly fed
Of that self-blood that first gave life to you,
And from that womb where you imprison'd were
He is enfranchised and come to light:
Nay, he is your brother by the surer side,
Although my seal be stamped in his face.

NURSE Aaron, what shall I say unto the empress?

DEMETRIUS Advise thee, Aaron, what is to be done,
And we will all subscribe to thy advice:
Save thou the child, so we may all be safe.

AARON Then sit we down, and let us all consult.
My son and I will have the wind of you:
Keep there: now talk at pleasure of your safety.

They sit

DEMETRIUS How many women saw this child of his?

AARON Why, so, brave lords! when we join in league,
I am a lamb: but if you brave the Moor,
The chafed boar, the mountain lioness,
The ocean swells not so as Aaron storms.
But say, again; how many saw the child?

NURSE Cornelia the midwife and myself;
And no one else but the deliver'd empress.

AARON The empress, the midwife, and yourself:
Two may keep counsel when the third's away:
Go to the empress, tell her this I said.

He kills the nurse

Weke, weke! so cries a pig prepared to the spit.

DEMETRIUS What mean'st thou, Aaron? wherefore didst thou this?

AARON O Lord, sir, 'tis a deed of policy:
Shall she live to betray this guilt of ours,
A long-tongued babbling gossip? no, lords, no:
And now be it known to you my full intent.
Not far, one Muli lives, my countryman;
His wife but yesternight was brought to bed;
His child is like to her, fair as you are:
Go pack with him, and give the mother gold,
And tell them both the circumstance of all;
And how by this their child shall be advanced,
And be received for the emperor's heir,
And substituted in the place of mine,
To calm this tempest whirling in the court;
And let the emperor dandle him for his own.
Hark ye, lords; ye see I have given her physic,

Pointing to the nurse

And you must needs bestow her funeral;
The fields are near, and you are gallant grooms:
This done, see that you take no longer days,
But send the midwife presently to me.
The midwife and the nurse well made away,
Then let the ladies tattle what they please.

CHIRON Aaron, I see thou wilt not trust the air
With secrets.

DEMETRIUS For this care of Tamora,
Herself and hers are highly bound to thee.

Exeunt DEMETRIUS *and* CHIRON *bearing off the Nurse's body*

AARON Now to the Goths, as swift as swallow flies;
There to dispose this treasure in mine arms,
And secretly to greet the empress' friends.
Come on, you thick lipp'd slave, I'll bear you hence;
For it is you that puts us to our shifts:
I'll make you feed on berries and on roots,
And feed on curds and whey, and suck the goat,
And cabin in a cave, and bring you up
To be a warrior, and command a camp.

Exit

SCENE-3— The same. A public place

Enter TITUS, *bearing arrows with letters at the ends of them; with him,* MARCUS, *Young* LUCIUS, PUBLIUS, SEMPRONIUS, CAIUS, *and other Gentlemen, with bows*

TITUS ANDRONICUS Come, Marcus; come, kinsmen; this is the way.
Sir boy, now let me see your archery;
Look ye draw home enough, and 'tis there straight.
Terras Astraea reliquit:
Be you remember'd, Marcus, she's gone, she's fled.
Sirs, take you to your tools. You, cousins, shall
Go sound the ocean, and cast your nets;
Happily you may catch her in the sea;
Yet there's as little justice as at land:
No; Publius and Sempronius, you must do it;
'Tis you must dig with mattock and with spade,
And pierce the inmost centre of the earth:
Then, when you come to Pluto's region,
I pray you, deliver him this petition;
Tell him, it is for justice and for aid,
And that it comes from old Andronicus,
Shaken with sorrows in ungrateful Rome.
Ah, Rome! Well, well; I made thee miserable
What time I threw the people's suffrages
On him that thus doth tyrannize o'er me.

Go, get you gone; and pray be careful all,
And leave you not a man-of-war unsearch'd:
This wicked emperor may have shipp'd her hence;
And, kinsmen, then we may go pipe for justice.

MARCUS ANDRONICUS
O Publius, is not this a heavy case,
To see thy noble uncle thus distract?

PUBLIUS
Therefore, my lord, it highly us concerns
By day and night to attend him carefully,
And feed his humour kindly as we may,
Till time beget some careful remedy.

MARCUS ANDRONICUS
Kinsmen, his sorrows are past remedy.
Join with the Goths; and with revengeful war
Take wreak on Rome for this ingratitude,
And vengeance on the traitor Saturnine.

TITUS ANDRONICUS
Publius, how now! how now, my masters!
What, have you met with her?

PUBLIUS
No, my good lord; but Pluto sends you word,
If you will have Revenge from hell, you shall:
Marry, for Justice, she is so employ'd,
He thinks, with Jove in heaven, or somewhere else,
So that perforce you must needs stay a time.

TITUS ANDRONICUS
He doth me wrong to feed me with delays.
I'll dive into the burning lake below,
And pull her out of Acheron by the heels.
Marcus, we are but shrubs, no cedars we
No big-boned men framed of the Cyclops' size;
But metal, Marcus, steel to the very back,
Yet wrung with wrongs more than our backs can bear:

And, sith there's no justice in earth nor hell,
We will solicit heaven and move the gods
To send down Justice for to wreak our wrongs.
Come, to this gear. You are a good archer, Marcus;

He gives them the arrows

'Ad Jovem,' that's for you: here, 'Ad Apollinem:'
'Ad Martem,' that's for myself:
Here, boy, to Pallas: here, to Mercury:
To Saturn, Caius, not to Saturnine;
You were as good to shoot against the wind.
To it, boy! Marcus, loose when I bid.
Of my word, I have written to effect;
There's not a god left unsolicited.

MARCUS ANDRONICUS Kinsmen, shoot all your shafts into the court:
We will afflict the emperor in his pride.

TITUS ANDRONICUS Now, masters, draw.

They shoot

O, well said, Lucius!
Good boy, in Virgo's lap; give it Pallas.

MARCUS ANDRONICUS My lord, I aim a mile beyond the moon;
Your letter is with Jupiter by this.

TITUS ANDRONICUS Ha, ha!
Publius, Publius, what hast thou done?
See, see, thou hast shot off one of Taurus' horns.

MARCUS ANDRONICUS This was the sport, my lord: when Publius shot,
The Bull, being gall'd, gave Aries such a knock
That down fell both the Ram's horns in the court;

	And who should find them but the empress' villain? She laugh'd, and told the Moor he should not choose But give them to his master for a present.
TITUS ANDRONICUS	Why, there it goes: God give his lordship joy!

Enter a Clown, with a basket, and two pigeons in it

	News, news from heaven! Marcus, the post is come. Sirrah, what tidings? have you any letters? Shall I have justice? what says Jupiter?
CLOWN	O, the gibbet-maker! he says that he hath taken them down again, for the man must not be hanged till the next week.
TITUS ANDRONICUS	But what says Jupiter, I ask thee?
CLOWN	Alas, sir, I know not Jupiter; I never drank with him in all my life.
TITUS ANDRONICUS	Why, villain, art not thou the carrier?
CLOWN	Ay, of my pigeons, sir; nothing else.
TITUS ANDRONICUS	Why, didst thou not come from heaven?
CLOWN	From heaven! alas, sir, I never came there God forbid I should be so bold to press to heaven in my young days. Why, I am going with my pigeons to the tribunal plebs, to take up a matter of brawl betwixt my uncle and one of the emperial's men.
MARCUS ANDRONICUS	Why, sir, that is as fit as can be to serve for your oration; and let him deliver the pigeons to the emperor from you.

TITUS ANDRONICUS Tell me, can you deliver an oration to the emperor
with a grace?

CLOWN Nay, truly, sir, I could never say grace in all my life.

TITUS ANDRONICUS Sirrah, come hither: make no more ado,
But give your pigeons to the emperor:
By me thou shalt have justice at his hands.
Hold, hold; meanwhile here's money for thy charges.
Give me pen and ink. Sirrah, can you with a grace
deliver a supplication?

CLOWN Ay, sir.

TITUS ANDRONICUS Then here is a supplication for you. And when you
come to him, at the first approach you must kneel,
then kiss his foot, then deliver up your pigeons, and
then look for your reward. I'll be at hand, sir; see
you do it bravely.

CLOWN I warrant you, sir, let me alone.

TITUS ANDRONICUS Sirrah, hast thou a knife? come, let me see it.
Here, Marcus, fold it in the oration;
For thou hast made it like an humble suppliant.
And when thou hast given it the emperor,
Knock at my door, and tell me what he says.

CLOWN God be with you, sir; I will.

TITUS ANDRONICUS Come, Marcus, let us go. Publius, follow me.

Exeunt

SCENE-4— The same. Before the palace

Enter SATURNINUS, TAMORA, DEMETRIUS, CHIRON, *Lords, and others;* SATURNINUS *with the arrows in his hand that* TITUS *shot*

SATURNINUS Why, lords, what wrongs are these! was ever seen
An emperor in Rome thus overborne,
Troubled, confronted thus; and, for the extent
Of egal justice, used in such contempt?
My lords, you know, as know the mightful gods,
However these disturbers of our peace
Buz in the people's ears, there nought hath pass'd,
But even with law, against the willful sons
Of old Andronicus. And what an if
His sorrows have so overwhelm'd his wits,
Shall we be thus afflicted in his wreaks,
His fits, his frenzy, and his bitterness?
And now he writes to heaven for his redress:
See, here's to Jove, and this to Mercury;
This to Apollo; this to the god of war;
Sweet scrolls to fly about the streets of Rome!
What's this but libelling against the senate,
And blazoning our injustice every where?
A goodly humour, is it not, my lords?
As who would say, in Rome no justice were.
But if I live, his feigned ecstasies
Shall be no shelter to these outrages:
But he and his shall know that justice lives
In Saturninus' health, whom, if she sleep,

He'll so awake as she in fury shall
Cut off the proud'st conspirator that lives.

TAMORA

My gracious lord, my lovely Saturnine,
Lord of my life, commander of my thoughts,
Calm thee, and bear the faults of Titus' age,
The effects of sorrow for his valiant sons,
Whose loss hath pierced him deep and scarr'd his heart;
And rather comfort his distressed plight
Than prosecute the meanest or the best
For these contempts.

Aside

Why, thus it shall become
High-witted Tamora to gloze with all:
But, Titus, I have touched thee to the quick,
Thy life-blood out: if Aaron now be wise,
Then is all safe, the anchor's in the port.

Enter Clown

How now, good fellow! wouldst thou speak with us?

CLOWN

Yea, forsooth, an your mistership be emperial.

TAMORA

Empress I am, but yonder sits the emperor.

CLOWN

'Tis he. God and Saint Stephen give you good den:
I have brought you a letter and a couple of pigeons here.

SATURNINUS *reads the letter*

SATURNINUS

Go, take him away, and hang him presently.

CLOWN

How much money must I have?

TAMORA

Come, sirrah, you must be hanged.

CLOWN

Hanged! by'r lady, then I have brought up a neck to a fair end.

Exit, guarded

SATURNINUS

Despiteful and intolerable wrongs!
Shall I endure this monstrous villany?

I know from whence this same device proceeds:
May this be borne?--as if his traitorous sons,
That died by law for murder of our brother,
Have by my means been butcher'd wrongfully!
Go, drag the villain hither by the hair;
Nor age nor honour shall shape privilege:
For this proud mock I'll be thy slaughterman;
Sly frantic wretch, that holp'st to make me great,
In hope thyself should govern Rome and me.

Enter AEMILIUS

What news with thee, AEmilius?

AEMILIUS
Arm, arm, my lord;--Rome never had more cause.
The Goths have gather'd head; and with a power
high-resolved men, bent to the spoil,
They hither march amain, under conduct
Of Lucius, son to old Andronicus;
Who threats, in course of this revenge, to do
As much as ever Coriolanus did.

SATURNINUS
Is warlike Lucius general of the Goths?
These tidings nip me, and I hang the head
As flowers with frost or grass beat down with storms:
Ay, now begin our sorrows to approach:
'Tis he the common people love so much;
Myself hath often over-heard them say,
When I have walked like a private man,
That Lucius' banishment was wrongfully,
And they have wish'd that Lucius were their emperor.

TAMORA
Why should you fear? is not your city strong?

SATURNINUS
Ay, but the citizens favor Lucius,
And will revolt from me to succor him.

TAMORA
King, be thy thoughts imperious, like thy name.

Is the sun dimm'd, that gnats do fly in it?
The eagle suffers little birds to sing,
And is not careful what they mean thereby,
Knowing that with the shadow of his wings
He can at pleasure stint their melody:
Even so mayst thou the giddy men of Rome.
Then cheer thy spirit : for know, thou emperor,
I will enchant the old Andronicus
With words more sweet, and yet more dangerous,
Than baits to fish, or honey-stalks to sheep,
When as the one is wounded with the bait,
The other rotted with delicious feed.

SATURNINUS But he will not entreat his son for us.

TAMORA If Tamora entreat him, then he will:
For I can smooth and fill his aged ear
With golden promises; that, were his heart
Almost impregnable, his old ears deaf,
Yet should both ear and heart obey my tongue.

To AEmilius

Go thou before, be our ambassador:
Say that the emperor requests a parley
Of warlike Lucius, and appoint the meeting
Even at his father's house, the old Andronicus.

SATURNINUS AEmilius, do this message honourably:
And if he stand on hostage for his safety,
Bid him demand what pledge will please him best.

AEMILIUS Your bidding shall I do effectually.

Exit

TAMORA Now will I to that old Andronicus;
And temper him with all the art I have,
To pluck proud Lucius from the warlike Goths.
And now, sweet emperor, be blithe again,
And bury all thy fear in my devices.

SATURNINUS Then go successantly, and plead to him.

Exeunt

ACT-5

SCENE-1 — Plains near Rome

Enter LUCIUS *with an army of Goths, with drum and colours*

LUCIUS

Approved warriors, and my faithful friends,
I have received letters from great Rome,
Which signify what hate they bear their emperor
And how desirous of our sight they are.
Therefore, great lords, be, as your titles witness,
Imperious and impatient of your wrongs,
And wherein Rome hath done you any scath,
Let him make treble satisfaction.

FIRST GOTH

Brave slip, sprung from the great Andronicus,
Whose name was once our terror, now our comfort;
Whose high exploits and honourable deeds
Ingrateful Rome requites with foul contempt,
Be bold in us: we'll follow where thou lead'st,
Like stinging bees in hottest summer's day
Led by their master to the flowered fields,
And be avenged on cursed Tamora.

ALL THE GOTHS

And as he saith, so say we all with him.

LUCIUS

I humbly thank him, and I thank you all.
But who comes here, led by a lusty Goth?

Enter a Goth, leading AARON *with his Child in his arms*

SECOND GOTH

Renowned Lucius, from our troops I stray'd
To gaze upon a ruinous monastery;
And, as I earnestly did fix mine eye

Upon the wasted building, suddenly
I heard a child cry underneath a wall.
I made unto the noise; when soon I heard
The crying babe controll'd with this discourse:
'Peace, tawny slave, half me and half thy dam!
Did not thy hue bewray whose brat thou art,
Had nature lent thee but thy mother's look,
Villain, thou mightst have been an emperor:
But where the bull and cow are both milk-
white,
They never do beget a coal-black calf.
Peace, villain, peace!'--even thus he rates
the babe,--
'For I must bear thee to a trusty Goth;
Who, when he knows thou art the empress'
babe,
Will hold thee dearly for thy mother's sake.'
With this, my weapon drawn, I rush'd upon
him,
Surprised him suddenly, and brought him
hither,
To use as you think needful of the man.

LUCIUS

O worthy Goth, this is the incarnate devil
That robb'd Andronicus of his good hand;
This is the pearl that pleased your empress'
eye,
And here's the base fruit of his burning lust.
Say, wall-eyed slave, whither wouldst thou
convey
This growing image of thy fiend-like face?
Why dost not speak? what, deaf? not a word?
A halter, soldiers! hang him on this tree.
And by his side his fruit of bastardy.

AARON

Touch not the boy; he is of royal blood.

LUCIUS

Too like the sire for ever being good.
First hang the child, that he may see it sprawl;
A sight to vex the father's soul withal.
Get me a ladder.

A ladder brought, which AARON *is made to ascend*

AARON Lucius, save the child,
And bear it from me to the empress.
If thou do this, I'll show thee wondrous things,
That highly may advantage thee to hear:
If thou wilt not, befall what may befall,
I'll speak no more but 'Vengeance rot you all!'

LUCIUS Say on: an if it please me which thou speak'st
Thy child shall live, and I will see it nourish'd.

AARON An if it please thee! why, assure thee, Lucius,
'Twill vex thy soul to hear what I shall speak;
For I must talk of murders, rapes and massacres,
Acts of black night, abominable deeds,
Complots of mischief, treason, villanies
Ruthful to hear, yet piteously perform'd:
And this shall all be buried by my death,
Unless thou swear to me my child shall live.

LUCIUS Tell on thy mind; I say thy child shall live.

AARON Swear that he shall, and then I will begin.

LUCIUS Who should I swear by? thou believest no god:
That granted, how canst thou believe an oath?

AARON What if I do not? as, indeed, I do not;
Yet, for I know thou art religious
And hast a thing within thee called conscience,
With twenty popish tricks and ceremonies,
Which I have seen thee careful to observe,
Therefore I urge thy oath; for that I know
An idiot holds his bauble for a god
And keeps the oath which by that god he swears,
To that I'll urge him: therefore thou shalt vow
By that same god, what god soe'er it be,
That thou adorest and hast in reverence,
To save my boy, to nourish and bring him up;
Or else I will discover nought to thee.

LUCIUS Even by my god I swear to thee I will.

AARON	First know thou, I begot him on the empress.
LUCIUS	O most insatiate and luxurious woman!
AARON	Tut, Lucius, this was but a deed of charity To that which thou shalt hear of me anon. 'Twas her two sons that murder'd Bassianus; They cut thy sister's tongue and ravish'd her And cut her hands and trimm'd her as thou saw'st.
LUCIUS	O detestable villain! call'st thou that trimming?
AARON	Why, she was wash'd and cut and trimm'd, and 'twas Trim sport for them that had the doing of it.
LUCIUS	O barbarous, beastly villains, like thyself!
AARON	Indeed, I was their tutor to instruct them: That codding spirit had they from their mother, As sure a card as ever won the set; That bloody mind, I think, they learn'd of me, As true a dog as ever fought at head. Well, let my deeds be witness of my worth. I train'd thy brethren to that guileful hole Where the dead corpse of Bassianus lay: I wrote the letter that thy father found And hid the gold within the letter mention'd, Confederate with the queen and her two sons: And what not done, that thou hast cause to rue, Wherein I had no stroke of mischief in it? I play'd the cheater for thy father's hand, And, when I had it, drew myself apart And almost broke my heart with extreme laughter: I pry'd me through the crevice of a wall When, for his hand, he had his two sons' heads; Beheld his tears, and laugh'd so heartily, That both mine eyes were rainy like to his :

And when I told the empress of this sport,
She swooned almost at my pleasing tale,
And for my tidings gave me twenty kisses.

FIRST GOTH
What, canst thou say all this, and never blush?

AARON
Ay, like a black dog, as the saying is.

LUCIUS
Art thou not sorry for these heinous deeds?

AARON
Ay, that I had not done a thousand more.
Even now I curse the day--and yet, I think,
Few come within the compass of my curse,--
Wherein I did not some notorious ill,
As kill a man, or else devise his death,
Ravish a maid, or plot the way to do it,
Accuse some innocent and forswear myself,
Set deadly enmity between two friends,
Make poor men's cattle break their necks;
Set fire on barns and hay-stacks in the night,
And bid the owners quench them with their tears.
Oft have I digg'd up dead men from their graves,
And set them upright at their dear friends' doors,
Even when their sorrows almost were forgot;
And on their skins, as on the bark of trees,
Have with my knife carved in Roman letters,
'Let not your sorrow die, though I am dead.'
Tut, I have done a thousand dreadful things
As willingly as one would kill a fly,
And nothing grieves me heartily indeed
But that I cannot do ten thousand more.

LUCIUS
Bring down the devil; for he must not die
So sweet a death as hanging presently.

AARON
If there be devils, would I were a devil,
To live and burn in everlasting fire,
So I might have your company in hell,
But to torment you with my bitter tongue!

LUCIUS
Sirs, stop his mouth, and let him speak no more.

Enter a Goth

THIRD GOTH — My lord, there is a messenger from Rome
Desires to be admitted to your presence.

LUCIUS — Let him come near.

Enter AEMILIUS — Welcome, AEmilius what's the news from Rome?

AEMILIUS — Lord Lucius, and you princes of the Goths,
The Roman emperor greets you all by me;
And, for he understands you are in arms,
He craves a parley at your father's house,
Willing you to demand your hostages,
And they shall be immediately deliver'd.

FIRST GOTH — What says our general?

LUCIUS — AEmilius, let the emperor give his pledges
Unto my father and my uncle Marcus,
And we will come. March away.

Exeunt

SCENE-2 — Rome. Before TITUS's house

Enter TAMORA, DEMETRIUS, *and* CHIRON, *disguised*

TAMORA

Thus, in this strange and sad habiliment,
I will encounter with Andronicus,
And say I am Revenge, sent from below
To join with him and right his heinous wrongs.
Knock at his study, where, they say, he keeps,
To ruminate strange plots of dire revenge;
Tell him Revenge is come to join with him,
And work confusion on his enemies.

They knock

Enter TITUS, *above*

TITUS ANDRONICUS

Who doth molest my contemplation?
Is it your trick to make me ope the door,
That so my sad decrees may fly away,
And all my study be to no effect?
You are deceived: for what I mean to do
See here in bloody lines I have set down;
And what is written shall be executed.

TAMORA

Titus, I am come to talk with thee.

TITUS ANDRONICUS

No, not a word; how can I grace my talk,
Wanting a hand to give it action?
Thou hast the odds of me; therefore no more.

TAMORA

If thou didst know me, thou wouldest talk with me.

TITUS ANDRONICUS	I am not mad; I know thee well enough: Witness this wretched stump, witness these crimson lines; Witness these trenches made by grief and care, Witness the tiring day and heavy night; Witness all sorrow, that I know thee well For our proud empress, mighty Tamora: Is not thy coming for my other hand?
TAMORA	Know, thou sad man, I am not Tamora; She is thy enemy, and I thy friend: I am Revenge: sent from the infernal kingdom, To ease the gnawing vulture of thy mind, By working wreakful vengeance on thy foes. Come down, and welcome me to this world's light; Confer with me of murder and of death: There's not a hollow cave or lurking-place, No vast obscurity or misty vale, Where bloody murder or detested rape Can couch for fear, but I will find them out; And in their ears tell them my dreadful name, Revenge, which makes the foul offender quake.
TITUS ANDRONICUS	Art thou Revenge? and art thou sent to me, To be a torment to mine enemies?
TAMORA	I am; therefore come down, and welcome me.
TITUS ANDRONICUS	Do me some service, ere I come to thee. Lo, by thy side where Rape and Murder stands; Now give me some surance that thou art Revenge, Stab them, or tear them on thy chariot-wheels;

And then I'll come and be thy waggoner,
And whirl along with thee about the globe.
Provide thee two proper palfreys, black as jet,
To hale thy vengeful waggon swift away,
And find out murderers in their guilty caves:
And when thy car is loaden with their heads,
I will dismount, and by the waggon-wheel
Trot, like a servile footman, all day long,
Even from Hyperion's rising in the east
Until his very downfall in the sea:
And day by day I'll do this heavy task,
So thou destroy Rapine and Murder there.

TAMORA

These are my ministers, and come with me.

TITUS ANDRONICUS

Are these thy ministers? what are they call'd?

TAMORA

Rapine and Murder; therefore called so,
Cause they take vengeance of such kind of men.

TITUS ANDRONICUS

Good Lord, how like the empress' sons they are!
And you, the empress! but we worldly men
Have miserable, mad, mistaking eyes.
O sweet Revenge, now do I come to thee;
And, if one arm's embracement will content thee,
I will embrace thee in it by and by.

Exit above

TAMORA

This closing with him fits his lunacy
Whate'er I forge to feed his brain-sick fits,
Do you uphold and maintain in your speeches,
For now he firmly takes me for Revenge;
And, being credulous in this mad thought,
I'll make him send for Lucius his son;
And, whilst I at a banquet hold him sure,

I'll find some cunning practise out of hand,
To scatter and disperse the giddy Goths,
Or, at the least, make them his enemies.
See, here he comes, and I must ply my theme.

Enter TITUS *below*

TITUS ANDRONICUS
Long have I been forlorn, and all for thee:
Welcome, dread Fury, to my woful house:
Rapine and Murder, you are welcome too.
How like the empress and her sons you are!
Well are you fitted, had you but a Moor:
Could not all hell afford you such a devil?
For well I wot the empress never wags
But in her company there is a Moor;
And, would you represent our queen aright,
It were convenient you had such a devil:
But welcome, as you are. What shall we do?

TAMORA
What wouldst thou have us do, Andronicus?

DEMETRIUS
Show me a murderer, I'll deal with him.

CHIRON
Show me a villain that hath done a rape,
And I am sent to be revenged on him.

TAMORA
Show me a thousand that have done thee wrong,
And I will be revenged on them all.

TITUS ANDRONICUS
Look round about the wicked streets of Rome;
And when thou find'st a man that's like thyself.
Good Murder, stab him; he's a murderer.
Go thou with him; and when it is thy hap
To find another that is like to thee,
Good Rapine, stab him; he's a ravisher.
Go thou with them; and in the emperor's court

There is a queen, attended by a Moor;
Well mayst thou know her by thy own proportion,
for up and down she doth resemble thee:
I pray thee, do on them some violent death;
They have been violent to me and mine.

TAMORA
Well hast thou lesson'd us; this shall we do.
But would it please thee, good Andronicus,
To send for Lucius, thy thrice-valiant son,
Who leads towards Rome a band of warlike Goths,
And bid him come and banquet at thy house;
When he is here, even at thy solemn feast,
I will bring in the empress and her sons,
The emperor himself and all thy foes;
And at thy mercy shalt they stoop and kneel,
And on them shalt thou ease thy angry heart.
What says Andronicus to this device?

TITUS ANDRONICUS
Marcus, my brother! 'tis sad Titus calls.

Enter MARCUS

Go, gentle Marcus, to thy nephew Lucius;
Thou shalt inquire him out among the Goths:
Bid him repair to me, and bring with him
Some of the chiefest princes of the Goths;
Bid him encamp his soldiers where they are:
Tell him the emperor and the empress too
Feast at my house, and he shall feast with them.
This do thou for my love; and so let him,
As he regards his aged father's life.

MARCUS ANDRONICUS
This will I do, and soon return again.

Exit

TAMORA
Now will I hence about thy business,
And take my ministers along with me.

TITUS ANDRONICUS
Nay, nay, let Rape and Murder stay with me;
Or else I'll call my brother back again,
And cleave to no revenge but Lucius.

TAMORA
[Aside to her sons] What say you, boys? will you
bide with him,
Whiles I go tell my lord the emperor
How I have govern'd our determined jest?
Yield to his humour, smooth and speak him fair,
And tarry with him till I turn again.

TITUS ANDRONICUS
[Aside] I know them all, though they suppose me mad,
And will o'erreach them in their own devices:
A pair of cursed hell-hounds and their dam!

DEMETRIUS
Madam, depart at pleasure; leave us here.

TAMORA
Farewell, Andronicus: Revenge now goes
To lay a complot to betray thy foes.

TITUS ANDRONICUS
I know thou dost; and, sweet Revenge, farewell.

Exit TAMORA

CHIRON
Tell us, old man, how shall we be employ'd?

TITUS ANDRONICUS
Tut, I have work enough for you to do.
Publius, come hither, Caius, and Valentine!

Enter PUBLIUS *and others*

PUBLIUS
What is your will?

TITUS ANDRONICUS
Know you these two?

PUBLIUS
The empress' sons, I take them, Chiron and Demetrius.

TITUS ANDRONICUS
Fie, Publius, fie! thou art too much deceived;

The one is Murder, Rape is the other's name;
And therefore bind them, gentle Publius.
Caius and Valentine, lay hands on them.
Oft have you heard me wish for such an hour,
And now I find it; therefore bind them sure,
And stop their mouths, if they begin to cry.

Exit

PUBLIUS, *& c. lay hold on* CHIRON *and* DEMETRIUS

CHIRON

Villains, forbear! we are the empress' sons.

PUBLIUS

And therefore do we what we are commanded.
Stop close their mouths, let them not speak a word.
Is he sure bound? look that you bind them fast.

Re-enter TITUS, *with* LAVINIA; *he bearing a knife, and she a basin*

TITUS ANDRONICUS

Come, come, Lavinia; look, thy foes are bound.
Sirs, stop their mouths, let them not speak to me;
But let them hear what fearful words I utter.
O villains, Chiron and Demetrius!
Here stands the spring whom you have stain'd with mud,
This goodly summer with your winter mix'd.
You kill'd her husband, and for that vile fault
Two of her brothers were condemn'd to death,
My hand cut off and made a merry jest;
Both her sweet hands, her tongue, and that more dear

Than hands or tongue, her spotless chastity,
Inhuman traitors, you constrain'd and forced.
What would you say, if I should let you speak?
Villains, for shame you could not beg for grace.
Hark, wretches! how I mean to martyr you.
This one hand yet is left to cut your throats,
Whilst that Lavinia 'tween her stumps doth hold
The basin that receives your guilty blood.
You know your mother means to feast with me,
And calls herself Revenge, and thinks me mad:
Hark, villains! I will grind your bones to dust
And with your blood and it I'll make a paste,
And of the paste a coffin I will rear
And make two pasties of your shameful heads,
And bid that strumpet, your unhallow'd dam,
Like to the earth swallow her own increase.
This is the feast that I have bid her to,
And this the banquet she shall surfeit on;
For worse than Philomel you used my daughter,
And worse than Progne I will be revenged:
And now prepare your throats. Lavinia, come,

He cuts their throats

Receive the blood: and when that they are dead,

Let me go grind their bones to powder small
And with this hateful liquor temper it;
And in that paste let their vile heads be baked.
Come, come, be every one officious
To make this banquet; which I wish may prove
More stern and bloody than the Centaurs' feast.
So, now bring them in, for I'll play the cook,
And see them ready 'gainst their mother comes.

Exeunt, bearing the dead bodies

SCENE-3 — Court of TITUS's house. A banquet set out

Enter LUCIUS, MARCUS, *and Goths, with* AARON *prisoner*

LUCIUS
Uncle Marcus, since it is my father's mind
That I repair to Rome, I am content.

FIRST GOTH
And ours with thine, befall what fortune will.

LUCIUS
Good uncle, take you in this barbarous Moor,
This ravenous tiger, this accursed devil;
Let him receive no sustenance, fetter him
Till he be brought unto the empress' face,
For testimony of her foul proceedings:
And see the ambush of our friends be strong;
I fear the emperor means no good to us.

AARON
Some devil whisper curses in mine ear,
And prompt me, that my tongue may utter forth
The venomous malice of my swelling heart!

LUCIUS
Away, inhuman dog! unhallow'd slave!
Sirs, help our uncle to convey him in.

Exeunt Goths, with AARON. *Flourish within*

The trumpets show the emperor is at hand.

Enter SATURNINUS *and* TAMORA, *with* AEMILIUS, *Tribunes, Senators, and others*

SATURNINUS
What, hath the firmament more suns than one?

LUCIUS What boots it thee to call thyself a sun?

MARCUS ANDRONICUS Rome's emperor, and nephew, break the parle;
These quarrels must be quietly debated.
The feast is ready, which the careful Titus
Hath ordain'd to an honourable end,
For peace, for love, for league, and good to Rome:
Please you, therefore, draw nigh, and take your places.

SATURNINUS Marcus, we will.

Hautboys sound. The Company sit down at table

Enter TITUS *dressed like a Cook,* LAVINIA *veiled, Young* LUCIUS, *and others.* TITUS *places the dishes on the table*

TITUS ANDRONICUS Welcome, my gracious lord; welcome, dread queen;
Welcome, ye warlike Goths; welcome, Lucius;
And welcome, all: although the cheer be poor,
'Twill fill your stomachs; please you eat of it.

SATURNINUS Why art thou thus attired, Andronicus?

TITUS ANDRONICUS Because I would be sure to have all well,
To entertain your highness and your empress.

TAMORA We are beholding to you, good Andronicus.

TITUS ANDRONICUS An if your highness knew my heart, you were.
My lord the emperor, resolve me this:
Was it well done of rash Virginius
To slay his daughter with his own right hand,
Because she was enforced, stain'd, and deflower'd?

SATURNINUS It was, Andronicus.

TITUS ANDRONICUS — Your reason, mighty lord?

SATURNINUS — Because the girl should not survive her shame,
And by her presence still renew his sorrows.

TITUS ANDRONICUS — A reason mighty, strong, and effectual;
A pattern, precedent, and lively warrant,
For me, most wretched, to perform the like.
Die, die, Lavinia, and thy shame with thee;

Kills LAVINIA

And, with thy shame, thy father's sorrow die!

SATURNINUS — What hast thou done, unnatural and unkind?

TITUS ANDRONICUS — Kill'd her, for whom my tears have made me blind.
I am as woful as Virginius was,
And have a thousand times more cause than he
To do this outrage: and it now is done.

SATURNINUS — What, was she ravish'd? tell who did the deed.

TITUS ANDRONICUS — Will't please you eat? will't please your highness feed?

TAMORA — Why hast thou slain thine only daughter thus?

TITUS ANDRONICUS — Not I; 'twas Chiron and Demetrius:
They ravish'd her, and cut away her tongue;
And they, 'twas they, that did her all this wrong.

SATURNINUS — Go fetch them hither to us presently.

TITUS ANDRONICUS — Why, there they are both, baked in that pie;
Whereof their mother daintily hath fed,
Eating the flesh that she herself hath bred.

'Tis true, 'tis true; witness my knife's sharp point.

Kills TAMORA

SATURNINUS Die, frantic wretch, for this accursed deed!

Kills TITUS

LUCIUS Can the son's eye behold his father bleed?
There's meed for meed, death for a deadly deed!

Kills SATURNINUS. *A great tumult.* LUCIUS, MARCUS, *and others go up into the balcony*

MARCUS ANDRONICUS You sad-faced men, people and sons of Rome,
By uproar sever'd, like a flight of fowl
Scatter'd by winds and high tempestuous gusts,
O, let me teach you how to knit again
This scatter'd corn into one mutual sheaf,
These broken limbs again into one body;
Lest Rome herself be bane unto herself,
And she whom mighty kingdoms court'sy to,
Like a forlorn and desperate castaway,
Do shameful execution on herself.
But if my frosty signs and chaps of age,
Grave witnesses of true experience,
Cannot induce you to attend my words,

To LUCIUS Speak, Rome's dear friend, as erst our ancestor,
When with his solemn tongue he did discourse
To love-sick Dido's sad attending ear
The story of that baleful burning night
When subtle Greeks surprised King Priam's Troy,
Tell us what Sinon hath bewitch'd our ears,
Or who hath brought the fatal engine in
That gives our Troy, our Rome, the civil wound.

My heart is not compact of flint nor steel;
Nor can I utter all our bitter grief,
But floods of tears will drown my oratory,
And break my utterance, even in the time
When it should move you to attend me most,
Lending your kind commiseration.
Here is a captain, let him tell the tale;
Your hearts will throb and weep to hear him speak.

LUCIUS

Then, noble auditory, be it known to you,
That cursed Chiron and Demetrius
Were they that murdered our emperor's brother;
And they it were that ravished our sister:
For their fell faults our brothers were beheaded;
Our father's tears despised, and basely cozen'd
Of that true hand that fought Rome's quarrel out,
And sent her enemies unto the grave.
Lastly, myself unkindly banished,
The gates shut on me, and turn'd weeping out,
To beg relief among Rome's enemies:
Who drown'd their enmity in my true tears.
And oped their arms to embrace me as a friend.
I am the turned forth, be it known to you,
That have preserved her welfare in my blood;
And from her bosom took the enemy's point,
Sheathing the steel in my adventurous body.
Alas, you know I am no vaunter, I;

My scars can witness, dumb although they are,
That my report is just and full of truth.
But, soft! methinks I do digress too much,
Citing my worthless praise: O, pardon me;
For when no friends are by, men praise themselves.

MARCUS ANDRONICUS Now is my turn to speak. Behold this child:

Pointing to the Child in the arms of an Attendant

Of this was Tamora delivered;
The issue of an irreligious Moor,
Chief architect and plotter of these woes:
The villain is alive in Titus' house,
And as he is, to witness this is true.
Now judge what cause had Titus to revenge
These wrongs, unspeakable, past patience,
Or more than any living man could bear.
Now you have heard the truth, what say you, Romans?
Have we done aught amiss,--show us wherein,
And, from the place where you behold us now,
The poor remainder of Andronici
Will, hand in hand, all headlong cast us down.
And on the ragged stones beat forth our brains,
And make a mutual closure of our house.
Speak, Romans, speak; and if you say we shall,
Lo, hand in hand, Lucius and I will fall.

AEMILIUS Come, come, thou reverend man of Rome,
And bring our emperor gently in thy hand,
Lucius our emperor; for well I know
The common voice do cry it shall be so.

ALL Lucius, all hail, Rome's royal emperor!

MARCUS ANDRONICUS Go, go into old Titus' sorrowful house,

To Attendants

And hither hale that misbelieving Moor,
To be adjudged some direful slaughtering death,
As punishment for his most wicked life.

Exeunt Attendants

LUCIUS, MARCUS, *and the others descend*

ALL Lucius, all hail, Rome's gracious governor!

LUCIUS Thanks, gentle Romans: may I govern so,
To heal Rome's harms, and wipe away her woe!
But, gentle people, give me aim awhile,
For nature puts me to a heavy task:
Stand all aloof: but, uncle, draw you near,
To shed obsequious tears upon this trunk.
O, take this warm kiss on thy pale cold lips,

Kissing TITUS

These sorrowful drops upon thy blood-stain'd face,
The last true duties of thy noble son!

MARCUS ANDRONICUS Tear for tear, and loving kiss for kiss,
Thy brother Marcus tenders on thy lips:
O were the sum of these that I should pay
Countless and infinite, yet would I pay them!

LUCIUS Come hither, boy; come, come, and learn of us
To melt in showers: thy grandsire loved thee well:
Many a time he danced thee on his knee,
Sung thee asleep, his loving breast thy pillow:
Many a matter hath he told to thee,
Meet and agreeing with thine infancy;
In that respect, then, like a loving child,

Shed yet some small drops from thy tender spring,
Because kind nature doth require it so:
Friends should associate friends in grief and woe:
Bid him farewell; commit him to the grave;
Do him that kindness, and take leave of him.

Young LUCIUS

O grandsire, grandsire! even with all my heart
Would I were dead, so you did live again!
O Lord, I cannot speak to him for weeping;
My tears will choke me, if I ope my mouth.

Re-enter Attendants with AARON

AEMILIUS

You sad Andronici, have done with woes:
Give sentence on this execrable wretch,
That hath been breeder of these dire events.

LUCIUS

Set him breast-deep in earth, and famish him;
There let him stand, and rave, and cry for food;
If any one relieves or pities him,
For the offence he dies. This is our doom:
Some stay to see him fasten'd in the earth.

AARON

O, why should wrath be mute, and fury dumb?
I am no baby, I, that with base prayers
I should repent the evils I have done:
Ten thousand worse than ever yet I did
Would I perform, if I might have my will;
If one good deed in all my life I did,
I do repent it from my very soul.

LUCIUS

Some loving friends convey the emperor hence,
And give him burial in his father's grave:
My father and Lavinia shall forthwith
Be closed in our household's monument.

As for that heinous tiger, Tamora,
No funeral rite, nor man m mourning weeds,
No mournful bell shall ring her burial;
But throw her forth to beasts and birds of prey:
Her life was beast-like, and devoid of pity;
And, being so, shall have like want of pity.
See justice done on Aaron, that damn'd Moor,
By whom our heavy haps had their beginning:
Then, afterwards, to order well the state,
That like events may ne'er it ruinate.

Exeunt

* * *

www.ingramcontent.com/pod-product-compliance
Lightning Source LLC
LaVergne TN
LVHW101925220826
846093LV00009B/375

* 9 7 8 9 3 5 4 6 2 7 5 8 3 *